PURITY CIRCLE WORKBOOK

friends helping friends live pure

By
Dora Isaac Weithers

TEACH Services, Inc.
Brushton, New York

2007 08 09 10 11 12 · 5 4 3 2 1

Copyright © 2005 Dora Isaac Weithers. All Rights Reserved.
Copyright © 2007 TEACH Services, Inc.
ISBN-13: 978-1-57258-472-3
ISBN-10: 1-57258-472-6

Published by

TEACH Services, Inc.
www.TEACHServices.com

CONTENTS

FOREWORD

Since becoming the Women's Ministries director for the Michigan Conference of Seventh-day Adventists in 1992, I have felt a need to be doing something more for younger women as we are charged in Titus 2. The Purity Circle program that Dora Weithers has developed is that answer. I wept as I read this manuscript wishing I'd had this guide and support when I was in my early teens.

God has blessed Dora with the unique ability to give us a thorough and practical Bible study on what it means to live a pure life style. This study is designed for both young and mature women of all religious preferences who want to live by God's principles for their lives.

In 1994 Dora conducted her first series of purity seminars at a weekend youth retreat in Texas. For the next ten years, hundreds of young men and women in Houston and the surrounding cities were led to commit to the purity lifestyle including sexual abstinence. According to Dora, "It bothered me that at each presentation we had so little time for such an important topic and there was no support system in place to help those who struggled with their commitment."

In 2004 while searching for a way to include the young women in her local church's Women's Ministries program, the Purity Circle idea was born. The Purity Circle concept is unique in that it creates a group who will provide long-term support to each other through both the good and the difficult times.

The workbook can be a useful tool for Women's Ministries groups who want to use the Purity Circle as a mentoring program. It can also be used by a mother who wants to encourage purity discussions with her daughter.

As Dora expresses it, "I have found that young women who say 'Yes' to godly womanhood are more empowered to say 'No' to the immoralities in our society. Purity Circle teaches the biblical principles which help them make wise decisions and it provides them with the support of 'friends helping friends live pure.'"

Myrna Earles, Director of Women's Ministries
Lake Union and Michigan Conferences of
Seventh-day Adventists

PREFACE

Ten-year-old Eva and her four friends strolled into the woods behind her house. Carrying small wicker baskets for their collection of wild flowers, they wandered off into different directions. The deeper into the woods they went, the farther they drifted away from each other.

Eva came upon a patch of lady slippers and was determined to leave them bare. She patiently stripped plant after plant, filling her basket with pink blossoms. She looked around for other patches of pink, but there were no more in sight. She did not look behind her. Unaware of the stranger who followed her cautiously, she walked forward.

Just when it seemed that Eva would not find any other flowers that were her favorite color, the stranger made deliberate heavy steps to attract her attention, and she looked back. He was carrying the most beautiful bouquet that she had ever seen.

"These are for you," he told her. "Here are all the colors that you like—not only pink. I can even show you to the area of the woods where they grow in abundance."

Keeping her eyes on the flowers—the blue bonnets, the white chamomiles with their yellow button centers, the clovers in various shades of pink—Eva walked toward him. Close up he had the kindest eyes and the most charming smile. Eva stared at him. Meanwhile with every breath she took, the strong aroma of the poisonous plants hidden between the pretty flowers sedated her. She began to feel like she was watching a fairy tale prince, who perhaps, could make her into a fairy tale princess.

He held out his right hand toward her and lowered the flowers in his left hand toward her basket. She stepped forward to receive the flowers.

"Eva!" she heard her name. The familiar voice broke her trance. Samantha, one of her friends, appeared and was surprised to find Eva communicating with a stranger—contrary to the warnings their parents had given them.

"Misty, Jodi, Karen!" Samantha shouted into the woods, "Come quickly!"

In her effort to respond to Samantha and the other girls who came running, Eva turned her back toward the stranger. Each of the other girls tried to position herself where she could see the faces of all the others and hear everything they had to say. Though not deliberate, they made a circle—the usual formation for group support.

"What were you doing, Eva?" Karen was always the one to make the others account for what they did.

Eva had tears in her eyes. Not until Samantha's voice jolted her back to reality did she realize that she had put herself in possible danger. She had almost wandered off with a complete stranger, and who knew what could have happened to her?

"Young lady, here are the flowers. You and your friends can enjoy them." The stranger's voice was so seductive that all the young women kept silent and listened.

Then Misty broke the silence. "We can enjoy our own flowers, thank you."

"Get away from us. Get away from Eva," added Jodi in a voice firmer than ever.

"And stay away!" stressed Karen.

As the girls filed past him on their way home, the stranger shook his head in disgust. Eva's friends had saved her from becoming his next victim. She had no idea that behind his charming smile, he had concealed some wicked intentions. The other girls did not know it either; they just did what they had to do in order to save their friend.

Like Eva, you know the difference between good and evil, and you desire to choose the good. However, temptation does not always present itself as an ugly, dangerous monster. Sometimes it comes bearing gifts—the very gifts you think you need. It can more easily deceive you when you walk alone.

Your challenge is not to know everything there is to know, but to maintain friendships with others who care enough to help you apply what you already know. By sharing love and concern in your Purity Circle, you will continue to learn from each other and help each other build your weaknesses into strengths.

Christ is at the center of your circle. The power to live pure lives comes from Him. As each of you draw near to Him for the power to live pure, you draw closer to each other, and your friendship bond strengthens and tightens to help keep impurity outside the circle.

These are the years when you create the memories that will last a lifetime. Let your Purity Circle friends help you to create happy memories that you will be glad to remember and proud to share.

Become part of the circle in which "friends help friends live pure"!

ACKNOWLEDGMENTS

Some wonderful people have been instrumental in promoting the Purity Circle Program and helping to provide this workbook. I am eternally grateful to:

Myrna Earles and Kimberly Purvis for their invaluable guidance, support, and time spent reading and re-reading.

The Michigan Conference of Seventh-day Adventists Women's Ministries Board for support beyond words.

The Lansing Purity Circle—Brittni, Christina, Jade and her sister Abby, Katie, Nia, Olivia and her sister Abby, Shanaisa and her sister Shalli, and Rose Nyakundi who willingly became test subjects for the material.

Nancy Khillah and others for contributing their valuable time and editing skills.

TEACH Services, Inc. for accepting and publishing the book.

My children, Wanda and Wendell, for encouraging me by their willingness to learn these principles.

God above all, who continues to bestow His gracious favor on the Purity Circle program.

Chapter 1

YOU HAVE BEEN CHOSEN

OBJECTIVES

(1)To make you aware that God has given you the power to live pure lives.
(2)To show that the purity lifestyle is best.

THEME TEXT

"Long ago, even before he made the world, God loved us and chose us in Christ to be holy and without fault in his eyes." (Ephesians 1:4.)

INTRODUCTION

Miss Teen Michigan and Miss Teen Ohio were the two finalists competing for the Miss Teen USA title in 2005. They held hands as they waited for the judges' decision. The envelope was opened and the winner was announced. Miss Teen Ohio was selected.

The crowed applauded. The Miss USA from a previous year crowned the new queen. She walked across the stage smiling with certainty that her life had been changed for the better.

Her mother had been a beauty queen in her teens, but that did not help the daughter to win the crown. The young woman was chosen because of her own physical beauty, her personal charm, and her personal skills. She had proven to the judges that she deserved to be chosen.

It is exciting to be honored for personal achievement! Every young woman deserves it, and God has such an experience planned for you.

He has chosen you to wear the title of holiness, which is a synonym for purity and genuine beauty. He is not asking you to walk across life's stage to be judged by your physique and talent. Those factors are important, but not as great as your decision to be a young woman "in Christ." (See theme text.) God wants you to become close friends with His Son, Jesus, who will be your companion in your purity walk. He will enable you to succeed in winning your crown.

Miss Teen USA will give up her crown after one year. She would not do justice to her title if she kept it forever. She will not always be a teen. Her physical beauty will fade. Her energy will diminish. She will eventually lose the poise that won her the position.

It is different with the young woman who wears the title of purity. Purity is spiritual and grows from the inside out. It is not put on like a costume, and it cannot be taken off on the outside. Purity becomes a lifestyle, and its rewards last forever.

God has chosen you for the purity lifestyle because:

(1) He wants you to represent Him.
(2) He wants you to experience the happiest life possible.
(3) He wants you to fulfill the purpose for which He made you.

This chapter discusses these three benefits of the purity lifestyle and reveals that it is God's great love which caused Him to design such a plan for you.

DISCUSSION

1. God wants you to represent Him.

a) How did God make the woman? Do you think there are special ways in which women can represent Him? Genesis 2:21, 22

_____

_____

_____

_____

At first God created one image. Then He separated that one image into two genders—male and female. It was clear that there would be some difference in the way the genders represent Him. As you discover your female uniqueness, you will discover unique ways in which God reveals Himself through you.

b) In what ways can young women represent Him? 1 Timothy 4:12

_____

_____

_____

_____

Even though older godly women make good teachers, young women make a greater impact on each other in matters of daily living. Your friends who do not listen to the older women will pay attention to you when you discuss topics like fashion, music, and body image. You have the opportunity to introduce other topics like purity. Do not underestimate your power of influence.

c) Why is it important to represent God during your youth? Ecclesiastes 12:1, 2

_____

_____

_____

_____

Youth is also the time when you make the decisions that affect your destiny. If you take the time now to cement your relationship with God, you invest in your happiness now and forever. If you procrastinate, you take the risk of living a dangerous life without Christ. Now is the time to give Him priority in your life. His companionship gives joyful meaning to the purity walk.

d) Does God love you whether or not you represent Him in the purity lifestyle? John 3:16; 1 John 4:9, 10

_____

_____

_____

_____

God loves you. It is His nature to love and He always will. He chose you hoping that you would choose Him too, because you enjoy His love more when you love Him. If a young man begins to pay attention to you, you will be excited to communicate with him if you like him. If you don't like him his attention may not matter. Similarly, when you learn to love God, you will appreciate the fact that He chose you.

2. God wants you to experience the happiest life possible.

a) How does one believer describe happiness in walking with the Lord? Psalms 16:11

_____

_____

_____

_____

The phrase "in Christ" as stated in our theme text is important. No matter what the circumstances are, your most important action is to cling to your relationship with Christ. He loves you and wants to help you maintain your happiness.

b) Cite one negative example of a woman who ruined the happy life God planned for her. Genesis 3:1–7

_____

_____

_____

_____

During creation week, God pronounced "good" on everything that He had made. The first thing that seemed "not good" was the fact that man was without human companionship, so God solved the problem by bringing the woman to him. Then the devil disturbed her pure thoughts with his fake wisdom on how to make her life better. Instead of making her good life better, she changed her life for the worse. You never have to disobey God in order to fulfill your desire for happiness.

c) Does God give second chances to women who misrepresent Him? Matthew 1:21, 22; 1 John 1:9

_____

_____

_____

_____

Whenever you think of how foolish Eve was to ruin her own happiness, think of how loving and forgiving God is. Eve's disobedience did not cause Him to give up on women. He used another woman, Mary, in His plan to bring into the world a Savior for everyone including Eve. Jesus came to be your Savior too. Whether it be a slight stain or the heavy grime of impurity on your character, He will forgive you. Admit your wrongdoing, repent, accept His forgiveness, and get close with Him again.

d) Cite one example of a woman who experienced the happiness God planned for her life. Luke 1:26–31

_____

_____

_____

_____

Mary described herself as the Lord's servant, and the angel said that God favored her. Whenever and wherever her story is told, it features the fact that she was a virgin. Her purity was an asset in her being chosen by God. Your purity will influence not only God's favor but also the respect you receive from your peers.

3. God wants you to fulfill the purpose for which He made you.

a) How do you know that God planned a specific purpose for you? Jeremiah 29:11

_____

_____

_____

_____

God spoke these words to the nation of Israel while they were in exile as a result of their rebellion. He was encouraging them to repent and restore their relationship with Him so that He could fulfill His original plan for them. He has the same desire for you. He knows that no one is capable of designing a nobler purpose than the one He has for you.

b) What steps can you take to discover your purpose? James 1:5; Psalms 32:8

_____

_____

_____

_____

God reveals His purpose through the dream He put within you. He has equipped you to pursue and fulfill it. Discover what your natural talents and spiritual gifts are. Ask your family members and peers to help point them out to you. Then think about what activities you enjoy doing, and what activities or performances bring you compliments. This is usually a good clue to your purpose.

As you mature your perspective might shift, but God's purpose for your life will continually reveal itself.

c) Cite one positive example of a woman who pursued and fulfilled God's purpose for her life. Esther 2:16, 17

_____

_____

_____

_____

The girl Esther became the young adult queen. Her physical beauty was a gift from God. It helped her to win the title of queen, but it was her beauty of character that saved her life. She was obedient to her cousin who raised her and faithful to the principles he taught her. The strength of her purity helped her overcome the struggles of life and to become a prominent figure in her nation's history.

d) Are there any promises that God will help you maintain purity and fulfill your purpose? 2 Peter 1:3, 4; Colossians 2:9, 10; Philippians 4:13

_____

_____

_____

_____

God has given you everything you need to succeed at the purity lifestyle. He has given you Christ who is the authority over all other authorities. If you choose to remain connected with Him, He shares with you His power to live victoriously.

POINTS TO REMEMBER

God has chosen you to live a pure lifestyle because:

a) He loves you.
b) He wants pure young women to represent Him.
c) You serve as a good example to other young women.
d) Purity now is a good investment for your future.
e) The purity lifestyle brings genuine happiness.
f) Pure living makes it easier to pursue and fulfill your purpose.

Chapter 2

UNDERSTANDING PURITY

OBJECTIVE

To explain that purity affects all areas of your life.

THEME TEXT

"How can a young person stay pure? By obeying your word and following its rules...I have hidden your word in my heart that I might not sin against you." Psalms 119:9, 11

INTRODUCTION

You've seen the orange juice advertisement. They use certain phrases to convince you that the juice is pure. No sugar added. No preservatives. No artificial flavor. According to them, the juice is the pure substance of the fruit. They sell cleanness which is an important element of purity.

They are confident that the juice is clean because it has been pasteurized. That means they have applied enough heat to remove any harmful bacteria that might have contaminated the fruit during harvesting. However, the same heat that destroys the bacteria also removes some enzymes and vitamins.

Now the juice is clean, but it is not complete because some nutrients are missing. Consumers have to make a choice. They can buy clean, pasteurized juice which lacks some of the original vitamins and enzymes. Or they can buy complete unpasteurized juice and risk drinking contamination.

Sometimes making choices in the purity lifestyle can be just as challenging. For example, do you hang out with the girlfriend who lends you good books to read but whose clothes reveal body parts that should be hidden? Or do you prefer to spend time with the one who is really kind and helpful but plays and sings only vulgar lyrics while she is helping? Purity is concerned with developing and keeping the virtues that you have.

The purity principle is this: the purity of Christ so drenches your heart that the heart spills purity into all areas of life—the thoughts, the attitudes, the conduct, and the relationships.

The purity lifestyle is challenging but enjoyable and rewarding. God specializes in empowering those who commit to walking in the right path. He gives instructions in His written word, His spoken word, and through His Holy Spirit in His communion with you. He enables you to live completely pure lives, demonstrating the whole fruit of His spirit,—"love, joy, peace, patience, kindness, goodness, faithfulness, gentleness, and self-control" (Galatians 5:22, 23).

He strengthens you to resist contamination—"sexual immorality, impure thoughts, eagerness for lustful pleasure, idolatry, participation in demonic activities, hostility, quarreling, jealousy, outbursts of anger, selfish ambition, divisions, the feeling that everyone is wrong except those in your own little group, envy, drunkenness, wild parties, and other kinds of sins" (Galatians 5:19–21).

In this chapter we will discuss how to apply the purity principles of cleanness and completeness to all areas of your lives including:

(1) Your thoughts.
(2) Your conduct.
(3) Your relationships.

DISCUSSION

1. Your Thoughts

a) What effect does your thinking have on the way you live? Romans 12:2

_____

_____

_____

_____

The text says that you can become a different person by changing the way you think. When a thought enters your mind, you can choose to nurture it, talk about it, and eventually act on it. If it comes from an evil source, it leads to evil action. If it comes from a godly source, it leads to godly action. So all your actions, pure or impure, begin with a thought. You become the young woman God designed you to be by developing the habit of nurturing only pure thoughts.

b) How can you prevent impure thoughts from developing in your mind? Psalms 119:9–11

_____

_____

_____

_____

Discarding an impure thought will not leave your mind blank. You have to replace it with a pure thought so that your mind will have something pure to work with. Bible promises and Bible affirmations are your best defense against evil thoughts.

Jesus illustrated this when the devil tempted Him to satisfy His appetite, to boost His own ego, and to engage in idolatry (Matthew 4:1–11). He recited appropriate Scripture which He had stored in his mind. Because He did not allow the devil's suggestion to gain access to His thoughts, He remained the same pure Jesus He was before His encounter with the devil.

c) What is the Scripture guideline for appropriate thinking? Philippians 4:8

_____

_____

_____

_____

Here the two parts of purity apply. Some thoughts may be complete with truth, but to share them would prove that discretion is missing. Others may be complete with "loveliness," but to act upon them when the time is not right would mean that good sense is missing. You will find that sometimes with God's help you correct your thinking just before you cross the line. When this happens smile and thank God for putting the right thought into your mind at the right time.

Items that feed thoughts opposite to the qualities mentioned in the verse are automatically put on a veto list. They include but are not limited to: pornography, indecent song lyrics, body piercing, provocative clothing, trashy books, movies which are explicit with sex and crime, suggestive e-mails, and smutty chat rooms.

d) How can you ensure that your mind is always open to Godly thoughts? Romans 8:5

_____

_____

_____

_____

In the morning before you start your day, give the control of your mind to God. His Spirit communicates with your spirit when you pray, when you read His Word, when you meditate on Him. Tell Him that you choose to listen to Him instead of ungodly sources, and ask Him for courage to obey what He says. Also, ask Him that when sudden situations occur, He will give you the wisdom to act upon principles that you have learned and stored.

2. Your Conduct

a) In what two categories do both the Old and New Testament writers place conduct —the way you live? How can you tell which category you belong to? Proverbs 9:6; Ephesians 5:15–17

_____

_____

_____

_____

God is the most qualified authority to judge what is wise and what is foolish. So, "Don't act thoughtlessly, but try to understand what the Lord wants you to do" (Ephesians 5:17).

b) What is God's counsel concerning deportment—the way you carry yourself? 1 Timothy 2:9, 10; 1 Peter 3:3, 4

_____

_____

_____

_____

The advice is not to neglect your outward appearance. It is rather that you do not dress to display your body and draw attention to it. Look beautiful. (Chapter Six will deal with dress in more detail.) Keep your motives clean and your virtues complete. Leave it to God to bring you to the attention of the right person at the right time. "The Lord will hold you in his hands for all to see — a splendid crown in the hands of God" (Isaiah 62:3).

c) What is His counsel concerning personal care — the way you treat your body? Romans 6:12, 13; Romans 12:1; 1 Thessalonians 4:3, 4

_____

_____

_____

_____

Self-respect has a prominent position in the purity lifestyle. You show your love and appreciation to God by taking care of His creation, your body. Giving your body completely to Him, includes but is not limited to: proper nutrition, appropriate exercise, rest, refraining from alcohol, nicotine, harmful drugs, and abstinence from premarital sex.

It is not only what pleases you, but more importantly, what pleases Him who made you.

d) What is His counsel concerning conversation—the things you talk about? Ephesians 5:4

_____

_____

_____

_____

You may have to talk less. However, that will give you time to think—to filter out the thoughts that are harmful and replace them with positive, motivational thoughts.

When you develop this habit, you'll speed up the process of becoming the woman God designed you to be.

3. Your Relationships

a) What attitude is repeated over and over in God's instructions for relating to others? What specific groups of people are mentioned? Leviticus 19:3, 14, 32; 1 Peter 2:17

_____

_____

_____

_____

Jesus in His sermon on the mount says, "Do for others what you would like them to do for you" (Matthew 7:12). Give to everyone, not only to the people you like, the respect that you want to receive from them.

b) How does God require holy people to relate to people who offend them? Colossians 3:12–14

_____

_____

_____

_____

Purity of thought, word, and action still apply even for difficult people. Kindness, patience, forgiveness, and all the other virtues come from God. We receive them from Him and pass them on to others. We share His complete purity, unspoiled by our prejudices.

c) Besides sexual abstinence, what else is important in premarital love relationships? 1 Corinthians 13:4–6

_____

_____

_____

_____

Sexual abstinence prior to marriage is only one aspect of purity in a love relationship. The kind of love described in the Bible also refrains from selfish behaviors like exploitation, rudeness, and lies. It does not cause emotional hurt. Pure love resembles God's love, and we can learn from Him. "For we know how dearly God loves us, because he has given us the Holy Spirit to fill our hearts with his love" (Romans 5:5).

God wants you to practice the purity principle in all aspects of your lives, in all your relationships, and His reward for you is one of high honor. "If you keep yourself pure, you will be a utensil God can use for his purpose. Your life will be clean, and you will be ready for the Master to use you for every good work" (2 Timothy 2:21). Your purity benefits both Him and you.

POINTS TO REMEMBER
a) Purity is comprised of completeness and cleanness.
b) The instructions for the purity lifestyle come from God.
c) Pure thinking is maintained by replacing evil thoughts with pure thoughts.
d) The purity lifestyle influences conduct and conversation.
e) Self-respect and respect for others are prominent in the purity lifestyle.
f) Purity includes but is not limited to sexual abstinence before marriage.

Chapter 3

CREATING THE CIRCLE

OBJECTIVE

To show the significance of the friendship circle in the purity lifestyle.

THEME TEXT

"I pray that your love for each other will overflow more and more, and that you will keep on growing in your knowledge and understanding. For I want you to understand what really matters, so that you may live pure and blameless lives until Christ returns." Philippians 1:9, 10

INTRODUCTION

You may have the opportunity to take the purity pledge when you complete the fifth Purity Circle session. The choice is yours. If you choose to pursue the purity lifestyle, you will commit to a pledge that thousands of young people have signed since the True Love Waits movement began in 1993. According to a research done by the Northern Kentucky University in 2003, almost half of those who signed pledges remained faithful. Some lacked the support to fulfill their good intention.

The Purity Circle was created to help improve the success ratio. Everyone has the opportunity to belong to the circle whether or not you pledge. If you have two or three friends here, you and your friends can choose to form a smaller circle within the large circle which means that you will keep closer watch over each other.

Although you do not think of it as a circle, you have purity support from your mother or female guardian, other members of your family as well as your teachers. They have been training you according to Titus 2:5 to "live wisely and pure." They were the first members of your Purity Circle. Now that you are old enough to select your friends, you can add to your circle those who will encourage you to uphold the purity principles you have been taught.

The concept of the circle is that the members face each other, connect with each other, affirm each other, and motivate each other to become the women God had in mind when He made each of you. Female friendship circles are good soil in which positive womanhood thrive and become productive. It is here that good women are empowered to become good wives, good mothers, or good career women.

The Purity Circle is also an appropriate forum for young women who have made early detours to re-establish their purity. In the circle members learn to observe and read each other's countenance. They offer sympathy and support to those who need it. The stronger members model their strengths and the weaker ones learn new strategies. The interest of one becomes the interest of all as you aim to succeed together.

The *Song of Solomon* supports the Purity Circle idea. The *Song* begins where Genesis left off in its presentation of human sexuality. Adam and Eve were created to supply companionship for each other, but not until the *Song* does the Bible exhibit the beauty of the love relationship between a man and a woman. As the lovers relate to each other, there is a group of friends whom we will call their Purity Circle, who give their input towards the happiness of the couple. We shall refer to them in our discussion.

Our theme text for this chapter is an appropriate prayer for each one to pray on behalf of the group. Whereas others have fallen because of peer pressure, you can, through God's grace, hold up each other by peer support.

We shall discuss three important features of the circle. At the end of this session, let your group leader know whether you already have friends for your inner circle or if you need help to create one.

(1)The composition
(2)The purpose
(3)The bond

DISCUSSION

1. The Composition

a) Who is the main source of spiritual and moral energy? To what extent is this source available? Psalms 121

_____

_____

_____

_____

God, through Christ, is the connecting link in the circle. If He is ignored the circle will not hold together. Remind each other as often as necessary to give Him priority in your individual lives and in the group.

b) How does the Bible describe those who desire to live holy lives? Psalms 24:3, 4; 2 Timothy 2:22

_____

_____

_____

_____

It makes sense to keep company with those who have the same interest. When all the members of the Purity Circle focus on developing godly womanhood, they appreciate the need to request and offer support when they meet their individual challenges.

c) What should be the attitude of the Purity Circle towards those who have visible signs of immorality but still want to be circle members? Colossians 3:12–14

_____

_____

_____

_____

Hopefully, young women who need the strength of the Purity Circle will comply with the practices of the group. Accept these young women. Look for their hidden strengths and ask God to show you how to build on them. We will discuss this in more detail in our chapter on *Little Sisters*.

2. Purpose

a) How is the Purity Circle in the *Song of Solomon* involved in the love relationship of the young woman? What does she ask them to do? What are they requesting from her? Song of Solomon 5:8, 9

_____

_____

_____

_____

The Purity Circle creates an atmosphere in which members feel comfortable to share their excitement as well as their problems. Make yourselves available to listen. Be accountable to each other so that you can help each other make wise decisions.

b) What commitment does the Purity Circle make to the young woman? Song of Solomon 6:1

_____

_____

_____

_____

_____

Purity Circle is committed to offering assistance. However, you may be struggling with a problem that no one notices. If this ever happens, bring your situation to the attention of someone. It is not wise to be secretive about your problem. One of the benefits of belonging to the Purity Circle is that it provides the love and concern of sisters who care.

c) What practice is very disruptive among friends who share their feelings? What commitment must each member make in order to avoid it? Proverbs 11:13; 16:28

_____

_____

_____

_____

Some girls say that gossip is the reason they prefer male rather than female friends. Truth is, gossip is not gender related; it occurs whenever and wherever people disregard the purity principles. As you develop into productive womanhood, you have the opportunity to help each other replace the desire for useless talk with the practice of talking hope and encouragement. You will discover the benefits of female friendships. You will learn to exercise trust in other women because you know that you deserve their trust.

d) What is the long-term goal of the Purity Circle? How long should this goal be in effect? Philippians 1:9, 10

_____

_____

_____

_____

Whether you get married or remain single, you can remain friends with your inner circle and make appropriate contributions towards the spiritual growth of each other. Prayer is always useful regardless of distance. An occasional e-mail, phone call, or postcard can also bring back good memories and inspire lifelong faithfulness.

3. The Bond

Larry Crabb,[1] uses the word "connecting" to describe what happens among a group or community who truly bond together. According to Larry, members connect with each other in the same way that God who is perfect reaches out and connects with the good in you.

- He accepts you for who you are while envisioning who you could be.
- He maintains His confidence about the good in you and remains merciful when your badness becomes visible.

- He exposes the bad in you only to demonstrate your need of His grace.

a) What attitude is necessary for you to benefit from your connecting? What is the result? Romans 15:5–7

_____

_____

_____

_____

Female bonding is not just a pastime. It is necessary for the sisterly support you need in your struggle against peer pressure. You walk in the direction opposite to the crowd when you pledge to a life of purity. Without your sisters (friends) beside you, you might be forced to choose between changing your course or getting trampled because you are alone in the crowd. You would not always have their physical presence, but you can count on their understanding, their cheers, and their prayers.

b) How do you demonstrate unity and mutual concern for each other? Whose life are you imitating when you do? Philippians 2:1–5

_____

_____

_____

_____

---

1   Crabb, Larry, *Connecting*, Word Publishing, Nashville, Tennessee, 1997.

As you build unity between each other, you demonstrate an important aspect of the life of Christ. Ellen White in *Adventist Home* gives a beautiful summary on the circle concept. "Picture a large circle, from the edge of which are many lines all running to the center. The nearer these lines approach the center, the nearer they are to one another. Thus it is in the Christian life. The closer we come to Christ, the nearer we shall be to one another. God is glorified as His people unite in harmonious action."

c) What is a good way to summarize your commitment to each other? 1 Thessalonians 5:11

_____

_____

_____

_____

This is a good time to find your inner circle and talk about your commitment to each other. In a later session on *Girlfriends*, we will discuss some issues that may arise within your long-term relationship, but right now, all that matters is your desire to commit and your willingness to look out for each other.

Enjoy your Purity Circle and help each other succeed in your purity walk.

POINTS TO REMEMBER
a) God is the main source of spiritual and moral energy for the Purity Circle.
b) The common goal of the Purity Circle is the purity lifestyle.
c) The Purity Circle creates an atmosphere in which members feel free to ask for help.
d) Purity Circle members practice love, forgiveness and unselfish support towards each other.
e) The Purity Circle affirms the positive power of female friendships.
f) The commitment to purity and the Purity Circle is for a lifetime.

Chapter 4

YOUR SOCIAL POSTURE

OBJECTIVE

To encourage each young woman to determine her own social standard.

THEME TEXT

"I am the rose of Sharon, the lily of the valley." Song of Solomon 2:1

INTRODUCTION

Abby's father died when she was a baby, so she and her mother lived with her grandmother until she was sixteen. The women took her to church regularly and taught her to love Jesus and His Word. During her teenage years she participated actively in the youth group and became a leader.

Everyone saw Abby as a godly, happy young woman with great potential. What they could not see was the inferiority and loneliness she felt when her friends talked about their fathers. She felt cheated whenever she listened to her friends talk about their interaction with their dads. She was grateful for the love and care which her mother and grandmother provided, but she longed to know what it was like to run into a father's arms, to hear a heavy male voice refer to her as "my daughter."

No wonder she developed a crush on the youth minister who was approachable and lavish in his admiration for her. Abby secretly wished to have him hold her hand or put his arms around her shoulder and walk her to the parking lot, the way some boys did with their girlfriends. Yet she knew that he would never think of her that way. He treated all the young people like he would his younger siblings.

She confided in her best friend Sallie, who discussed it with her mom, who thought it wise to inform Abby's grandmother, who took the responsibility to help Abby sort out her feelings.

"Feelings are important," her grandmother said over dinner, "but even more important is the way you feel about yourself."

She expected Abby to know, without her mentioning it directly, that she was talking about Abby's admiration for the youth minister. Somehow Abby realized it, so she listened.

"What you think about yourself determines how you relate to other people and how you expect them to relate to you. You are a beautiful and talented young lady, special to God, to your mother, and to me. We love you. You are our gift from Him, and we want you to think about yourself in that same way."

"Yea," Abby thought to herself. "They love me, and I love them too, but they are women. Don't I get to love a man?"

"It is normal for a young woman to crave the affection of a man." Her grandmother seemed to have read her thoughts. "It proves that she is emotionally healthy. However, controlling her feelings proves that she is spiritually and morally healthy. God designed you to fulfill an important purpose in His scheme of things. He will bring you love that will inspire you, not embarrass you, and He will bring it to you at the appropriate time."

"You really believe that God will bring love to me, Grandma?"

"It's for you to believe. If you love Him enough, and trust Him enough to provide for all your needs, then expect Him to be interested in your love life also."

Abby's grandmother touched on some issues that are essential to the self-esteem of a godly young woman. They will form the basis of our discussion in this lesson, and the love relationship in the Song of Solomon will be our main reference.

(1) Know who you are
(2) Know the kind of love you deserve
(3) Be patient

DISCUSSION

1. Know who you are

a) How does the young woman in the Song of Solomon refer to herself? What thoughts come to your mind concerning the metaphors she uses? Song of Solomon 2:1

_____

_____

_____

_____

Sharon is a low-lying valley region in North Palestine between Mount Tabor and Lake Tiberias. The rose from Sharon is as beautiful as any other rose; the lily is as pure as any other lily, even though these flowers grow in the valley as opposed to the mountaintop on which their beauty can be conspicuous. Beauty is modest, not arrogant. Jesus expressed this attitude of humility when He said, "I am meek and lowly in heart" (Mathew 11:29 KJV).

b) What do you think of the figurative language used by the Psalmist to describe godly young women? Psalms 144:12

_____

_____

_____

_____

c) Create your own metaphor to describe who you are, and explain it. If you choose
   to adopt one of the biblical symbols as your own, explain why.

_____

_____

_____

_____

No matter how other people describe you, what matters most is how you describe yourself. You determine who you are based on who God says you are. You
have the right to insist that other people relate to you in a way that is appropriate
to your self-image. Make it a habit to mentally reaffirm who you are when your
image is threatened. Soon your attitude, your deportment, and your expressions
will automatically reflect who you are.

2. Know the kind of love you deserve

a) How does the young man in the Song of Solomon respond to the young woman's
   description of herself? Why is his response important? Song of Solomon 2:2

_____

_____

_____

If your friends accept that you are who you say you are, they will try to meet
your expectations in their relationship with you.

b) What kind of love is to be expected from a godly young man who thinks highly
   of his female friend? 1 Corinthians 13:4–7

_____

_____

_____

_____

You deserve love that compares with this biblical model. It is not too much to ask for, and it is not too much for you to give.

c) What does the young woman in the *Song of Solomon* think about her male friend? What do you think about the metaphors she uses to describe him? Song of Solomon 2:3

_____

_____

_____

_____

Do you feel respected and validated in the company of your male friend? Are you empowered by his comments, by his interaction with you and with his other friends? What makes you consider him "the finest"? It is important that you evaluate him based on what you see, not on changes you hope for.

3. Be patient

a) What advice does the young woman in the *Song of Solomon* give to her girlfriends? How would you respond to this advice from your friends in your Purity Circle? Song of Solomon 2:7

_____

_____

_____

_____

Being in a love relationship is exciting, and is more enjoyable if the timing is right. The decisions to commit to a relationship with Christ and the decision to discover and pursue the vocation God has called you to will improve your chances for a happy love relationship. When you know who you are and where you're heading, you will be able to choose friends who are traveling in the same direction. They will understand your commitment to the purity lifestyle, which includes sexual abstinence until a biblical marriage.

Joshua Harris in *I Kissed Dating Goodbye*, suggests that one on one relationships are not necessary for young people until they are mature enough to make a commitment. Why expose yourself to temptation and create struggles which frustrate you? The young woman in the Song is telling her friends not to arouse feelings that they know they cannot satisfy.

b) What is the value of being patient even when the temptation is strong? How can you use this advice with reference to the metaphor you have created to describe yourself? James 1:3, 4

_____

_____

_____

_____

If you refuse to force open the rose and the lily, they will last longer. Whatever metaphor you choose, you will find that maturity takes time.

c) Here is a beautiful passage that has been circulating for sometime among promoters of the purity lifestyle. The author has not been identified. Personalize it, and ask God to help you let this be a description of your moral and social posture.

"Everyone longs to give himself completely to someone, to have a deep soul relationship with another, to be loved thoroughly and exclusively.

"But God, to a believer, says:

'No, not until you are satisfied, fulfilled, and content with being loved by Me alone, until giving yourself totally to me, to have an intensely personal and unique relationship with Me alone, discovering that only in Me is your satisfaction to be found, will you be capable of the perfect human relationship that I have planned for you.'

'You will never be united with another until you are united with Me, exclusive of any other desires or longings.'

'*I want you to stop planning, stop wishing, and allow Me to give you the most thrilling plan existing—one that you cannot imagine! I want you to have the best.*'

'Please allow Me to bring it to you. You just keep watching Me, expecting the greatest things. Keep experiencing the satisfaction that I Am. Keep listening and learning the things I tell you. You just wait, that's all.'

'Don't be anxious. Don't look at the things you want. You just keep looking up to Me, or you'll miss what I want to show you! And then when you are ready, I'll surprise you with a love far more wonderful than you could dream of.'

'*You see, until you are ready—I am working even this moment to have both of you ready at the same time—until you are both satisfied exclusively with Me and the life I have prepared for you, you will not be able to experience the love that exemplifies your relationship with Me, and this perfect love.*'

'And dear one, I want you to have the most wonderful love. I want you to see in the flesh a picture of your relationship with Me and to enjoy materially and concretely the everlasting union of beauty, perfection, and love that I offer you with Myself.'

'Know that I love you utterly. I am the Almighty God. Believe it and be satisfied!'"

POINTS TO REMEMBER

a) You owe it to yourself to create a mental self-portrait.
b) You deserve friends who accept what you think about yourself.
c) It is emotionally healthy for young women to desire male affection.
d) Patience is essential when forming male-female relationships.
e) You deserve love that compares with the biblical model.
f) An intimate relationship with God improves your chances for a happy male-female relationship.

Chapter 5

PRIVATE GARDENS

OBJECTIVE

To affirm that sexual purity increases the joy in premarital relationships.

THEME TEXT

"You are like a private garden, my treasure, my bride! You are like a spring that no one else can drink from, a fountain of my own." Song of Solomon 4:12

INTRODUCTION

Marsha and Mark belonged to the same youth choir at church and they shared the same basketball coach at school. They saw each other and talked often. The rumor was that he liked her, but he never showed any personal interest when they were together. She liked him on the basketball court, but she never considered him a serious candidate for her affections.

Mark called regularly, but his conversations were never intimate. They talked about choir music, about the games, and about the weather. Neither did he ever ask her out.

Marsha missed the game that qualified the boys for the season play-off. The next day he invited her to come watch the videotape at his apartment. Since he had never crossed the line in his conversations, she had no reason to believe that he had any hidden motives, so she agreed. It did not bother her that he was home alone.

She was surprised that there was no basketball on the video that was playing when she entered the room. There were nude people and she preferred not to watch. She asked that he change the video. He did so with lots of apologies. He said that he had put that tape in by accident.

Eventually, he found the correct tape and set it up. He sat on the couch beside her. During each throw of the ball and each applause, he got closer. Marsha became uncomfortable and warned him about getting in her space.

"What's the matter? Can't I touch you?"

"Excuse me. You and I aren't the kind of friends who touch each other." She tried to be calm.

"Well, I'd like to be that kind of friend. Don't you enjoy my company?"

"Thanks, but no thanks," said Marsha, rising to leave.

Mark grabbed her and tried to wrestle her back onto the couch. She was stronger than he realized, and she managed to get out of the apartment. She left feeling stupid and ashamed. She knew that if she ever spoke about this incident she was likely to be questioned about being alone with him. Her friends would think that she was dumb for not suspecting the motives behind his many calls. She had not been harmed physically, but she felt violated.

The young woman in the Song of Solomon referred to herself as a rose (2:1). Continuing the metaphor, her lover later refers to her as a private garden (4:12). Roses are for spectators to admire, not to handle callously or to analyze as experiments.

Young women's emotions are as fragile as the rose. They bruise easily and need loving, gentle care. God in His wisdom requires that the garden be closed so that the public can view and admire, but not get close enough to trespass and litter. This chapter deals with:

(1) The Garden
(2) Garden Intruders
(3) Garden Fruits

1. The Garden

a) What symbols does the lover in the *Song* use to describe his virgin bride? Song of Solomon 4:12

_____

_____

_____

_____

Imagine how special it makes him feel that his bride has been untouched by anyone else. Imagine how satisfied she must be to express her love for her husband in a way that she has expressed it to no one else.

b) What commitment can a young woman make first that will strengthen her to keep her body pure for her future spouse? Romans 12:1; 1 Corinthians 6:19, 20

_____

_____

_____

_____

c) Considering all that you have learned so far, write at least three personal affirmations that you can repeat if you are tempted to engage in premarital sex. Your past does not matter. This is a new day and a new beginning.

_____

_____

_____

_____

_____

_____

_____

_____

The young woman symbolized by the private garden is enclosed by the presence and the power of God for her safety. She is not shut in to lessen her fun; but to protect her and preserve her for the ultimate joy at the appropriate time. The choice to keep your garden private is a choice that God honors. You'll be proud of your choice when you meet the gardener who commits to cherishing you for a lifetime.

2. Garden Intruders

Continuing the garden symbol, the male in the relationship would be the gardener.

a) What is an appropriate biblical guideline for selecting your male friends? 2 Timothy 2:22

_____

_____

_____

_____

Mark in our introductory story would be disqualified as a candidate for a special friendship. He is a good example of a garden intruder.

b) How did the first garden intruder seduce his first victim? Genesis 3:4–6

_____

_____

_____

_____

First, the devil convinced Eve that she lacked something—wisdom. Then he offered to fulfill that need. Garden intruders follow in his steps, offering you fake love that can result in other offers you don't need—like pregnancies, STDs, and addictions that can change your life forever. They sometimes catch you off guard because they do not present themselves as taking something from you, but rather as giving you something you lack. They pretend to improve you. They cannot. Only the God who made you can totally satisfy you.

You can never be too cautious about intruders. They intrude on your physical space. They also intrude on your thinking. They try to have you adopt their ideas as your own. Counsel with your Purity Circle members when in doubt.

c) What essential element will enable the garden to keep its door locked when intruders come around? Psalms 119:9-11; 1 Corinthians 10:13

_____

_____

_____

_____

Like Marsha, some young women are caught off guard, but their determination to purity empowers them to stand strong. Sharing that determination with the members of your Purity Circle will double your strength.

3. Garden Fruits

a) How is the garden symbol continued in the man's expression to his lover in the *Song*? Song of Solomon 4:13, 14

_____

_____

_____

_____

All his senses are satisfied with the completeness of her purity. She is totally pleased with herself for maintaining her purity. According to the Bible commentaries all the spices mentioned carry pleasant fragrances. The mandrakes are "love apples" supposed to enliven the spirits and excite love. The wedding night is worth waiting for, when two people can enjoy each other in the bliss of true love.

b) How else is the fruit borne by godly women described? How does it compare with the fruits mentioned above? Galatians 5:22, 23

_____

_____

_____

_____

God wants the godly woman to satisfy His senses with the sight and fragrance of godly virtues. These characteristics also attract the man who is interested in a young woman committed to the purity lifestyle.

c) What practical fruits can the older women teach the younger women to produce? Titus 2:4, 5

_____

_____

_____

_____

Your extended Purity Circle can include motherly figures who can help you mature into outstanding models of godly womanhood among your contemporaries. Gardens must be as functional as they are beautiful.

POINTS TO REMEMBER
a) Godly young women are like private gardens to be admired, not explored.
b) God dwells in your body; it is holy.
c) Choose male friends who respect holiness, including your body.
d) Garden intruders lie when they offer to improve you; only God can.
e) The Word of God inside you makes you stand firm against temptations.
f) Good gardens bear good fruit, the spiritual fruit of God's Spirit and the practical fruit of productive womanhood.

Chapter 6

YOU ARE SO BEAUTIFUL

OBJECTIVES

(1)To help you understand the importance of appropriate clothing in the purity lifestyle.

(2)To point out that your beauty is exhibited by you, not by your clothing.

THEME TEXT

"And I want women to be modest in their appearance. They should wear decent and appropriate clothing and not draw attention to themselves by the way they fix their hair or by wearing gold or pearls or expensive clothes." 1 Timothy 2:9

INTRODUCTION

Appearance is super-important. God wants your admirers to see that purity in a young woman is attractive and beautiful. You prove this truth to them by the way you present yourself.

For the godly woman, beauty and purity are synonymous. They are put forth from the character on the inside, not put on in the clothes you wear. So even though you choose clothing that highlights your hair and eye colors, and compliments your size and shape, remember that it is your character that determines your beauty.

Your clothes, however, advertise the content of your character just like the candy wrapper advertises the brand and the ingredients. Clothing tells whether the body inside belongs to a young woman who respects or disrespects herself. It tells whether she cares to protect the privacy of her body or is careless to expose it for all to see.

If the wrapper on a chocolate candy bar comes loose, some shoppers will pinch it and taste it just because it is exposed. Some will take their pinch because they are curious, others just because they like free stuff. That candy bar is doomed to become an unwanted item. The pinchers will not buy what they have tasted for free, and the other shoppers who are honest and health-conscious will choose candy bars which are still fully wrapped.

Similarly if you loosen your clothing wrappers, you will attract males who want to explore and move on to the next free sample. If you wear clothes that protect your privacy, you will attract friends who respect you for respecting yourself.

Of course, there is the argument that males should focus on good thoughts and not be tempted by what the women wear. However, men cannot ignore your body image forever. They look at you when they greet you, and it is natural for them to admire you when you walk by. If you expose body parts that they do not expect to see, curiosity will make them look again. Then their brains signal their testosterone to respond.

Generally they respond according to their conviction, or lack of it. Males who have not subscribed to the purity lifestyle will try to obey their physical urges to reach out and touch whenever the opportunity presents itself. Those who are committed to purity will fight to control their feelings. This second group usually encourages young women not to contribute to the man's physical struggles by dressing carelessly. They will respect you for your modesty.

Remember how the gardener in the last chapter appreciated the fact that his young bride had remained a private garden. Whether or not you become a bride, your beauty of character will be enhanced by your decision not to expose the private parts of your body. You maintain your full worth when you remain fully wrapped; when the wrapper loosens, shoppers expect to receive discounts. God has put a high price on you. It is your responsibility to maintain it.

In this chapter you will see that God also requires this attitude of privacy, especially in the worship setting. You will be encouraged to set your own dress standards pleasing to God, to the godly people around you who care, and to your self. Purity Circle members can help each other adhere to the purity principle in your dress habits.

Whatever standards you set, there are three words in our theme text that you will want to include. This chapter will discuss dress using these words in our subtopics:
(1) Modest
(2) Decent
(3) Appropriate

DISCUSSION

1. Modest

a) What purpose for dressing is **not** in keeping with the principle of modesty? 1 Peter 3:3, 4

_____

_____

_____

_____

In 2000, pop star Britney Spears began to promote the purity lifestyle. Although she did not smoke, drink, or engage in premarital sex, many people did not take her seriously. They were offended by her almost nude appearances, exposing parts of her body that should have been covered. She soon fell off the purity wagon and gave in to other immoral acts.

Purity includes modesty. "Modesty" is a synonym for "humility" and "reserve." It is not showy. God gave you a beautiful body to be cherished and nurtured; not to be exhibited like a candy without a wrapper. Modest clothing sends the message that you appreciate the worth God placed on your body; that you consider it too valuable for public display. Rather, show your cheerful smile and your good manners. Wear clothing that validates your good sense.

b) What benefits the godly woman more than physical beauty? Proverbs 31:30

_____

_____

_____

_____

It is the synthetic beauty that fades. When the mature woman's hair begins to thin and her face becomes wrinkled, she begins to think of herself as less beautiful only if she judges her beauty by her looks. Although she may no longer wear the latest fashions, the godly woman grows more beautiful as her character develops. Her beauty of character cannot be erased by changes in her appearance. Young women who concentrate on purity in their lifestyles also develop a beauty of character that outlasts their youthful charm. Your peers will always remember you for your moral support. People outside your immediate circle of friends will admire your integrity. God will honor you—forever.

c) Rather than being known for your outward beauty, what is it better to be known for? 1 Peter 3:3, 4

_____

_____

_____

_____

"The best and most beautiful things in the world cannot be seen, nor touched… but are felt in the heart," said Helen Keller (1880–1968). She knew firsthand about beauty that is not seen but felt. She became blind and deaf in her childhood but managed to secure a place in the National Women's Hall of Fame. She is remembered for her efforts to help other blind people. She is an example of a quiet and gentle spirit which God considers very precious.

Choose friends that admire you for your intelligence and good nature rather than your clothes. God puts the priority on character, and godly friends will do the same.

2. Decent

a) What is the biblical principle on decency? Romans 13:13, 14

_____

_____

_____

_____

Modesty is the principle that determines how you choose your clothes. Decency has to do with the way your appearance, like your conduct, affects other people.

If a Purity Circle sister comes to visit one morning before you get out of bed, she might knock on your door and ask, "Are you decent?" It is important that she sees you the way you want her to see you. You might put on your robe rather than open the door in your skimpy pajamas. That's decency.

It is your responsibility to dress decently in the company of other people. Are your male friends seeing more than is modest to show? If so, you are indecent. The text mentions some serious immoral activities that are associated with indecency. When you dress indecently, you invite trouble and may not always be able to avoid the consequences.

b) How did God show His concern for decency in the worship service? Is this applicable today when you dress for church? Exodus 20:26

_____

_____

_____

_____

God did not want the members of the congregation to see the priest's underwear as he climbed the stairs. That would not be decent.

Nowhere is decency more important than in the presence of God. He knows what you look like when you're naked, but His concern is for the people who gather to worship Him. They should not be distracted.

It is not so unusual these days to see underwear and thighs because the slit in the side or back of the skirt is too high, or the waist is too low, and the blouse is too short. Sometimes the shape and the color of the underwear are obvious because the material makes it easy to see through, or the clothes fit too tightly. This is indecent anywhere; but in the holy atmosphere of worship, it is disgraceful.

Modesty and decency in your worship attire testify to your beauty of character. You display elegance and dignity when your clothes fit rightly, not tightly. You reveal maturity and good taste which are admirable qualities in a young woman.

3. Appropriate

a) What emphasis did Jesus put on the right clothes for the right occasion? Matthew 22:11–14

_____

_____

_____

_____

Some clothes may be decent but still out of place for the occasion. Showing up at a wedding in a modest gym suit shows disregard for the bride and groom and for social standards. It says that you have poor taste. The same thing can be said when you show up for worship looking like you are dressed for the playground. Modest jeans or shorts may be appropriate for an afternoon stroll, and still not be appropriate for church. It is not about the cost of what you wear, it is about respect for God, for others, and for yourself.

Way back in Old Testament times people dressed according to the event. The Bible mentions traveling clothes (Exodus 12:11), mourning clothes (2 Samuel 14:2), party clothes (Isaiah 3:22), and more. The practice of dressing appropriately still applies. We still guess who people are and where they are going based on how they are dressed.

b) In Solomon's description of a prostitute, what is the first thing about her appearance to identify her? Proverbs 7:6–10

_____

_____

_____

_____

It would be embarrassing for a young woman to be considered a prostitute or any other immoral character when she does not think of herself that way. Yet, whether or not you believe it, people watch you and form opinions based on the way you dress.

Thirteen-year-old Jan walked into the store with her friends after school. They pressured her into her first shoplifting experience. She had never done this before and never would have done it on her own. She tried to explain this to the cop when he threatened to arrest her and the others, but the cop did not believe her.

When Jan's mother went to pick her up at the jail, the cop explained, "Ma'am, it was hard to convince me that she was as well behaved as she said she was. The young women who wear tattoos and pierce their bodies are troublemakers. When I saw that ring in her nose and that tattoo on her arm, nothing she said could make me believe that she was not just another delinquent."

Certain styles of fashion correspond with certain styles of behavior. Outrageous colors in make-up, extravagant hairstyles, and excessive accessories are inappropriate for the modest young woman.

c) When God chose Aaron for the priesthood, what instructions did He give about the way he should dress? Exodus 28:2, 3

_____

_____

_____

_____

God wanted everyone to know from Aaron's special clothing that he was chosen to represent Him. God has chosen you for the purity lifestyle, and He wants you to dress according to His standards so that everyone will recognize the beauty and holiness of a godly young woman.

God made you beautiful and chose you to live pure. Paul gives some wise counsel in Colossians 3:12, 14. "Since God chose you to be the holy people whom he loves, you must clothe yourselves with tenderhearted mercy, kindness, humility, gentleness, and patience…And the most important piece of clothing you must wear is love. Love is what binds us all together in perfect harmony. "

When you wear this clothing on the inside, you will choose modest, decent, and appropriate clothing on the outside. You will be most beautiful.

POINTS TO REMEMBER
a. Your beauty is displayed in your character, not in your clothes.
b. Your clothing reveals the brand and the ingredients of your character.
c. Godly males appreciate young women who dress modestly.
d. Modest dress can be appropriate for some occasions but not appropriate for worship.
e. Modesty and decency in worship is God's requirement.
f. Beauty of character outlasts beauty of fashion.

Chapter 7

THE LITTLE FOXES

OBJECTIVES
(1) To explain that desirable elements in the love relationship can become either productive or destructive.
(2) To show that the purity principle makes the difference for good.

THEME TEXT
"Quick! Catch the little foxes before they ruin the vineyard of your love, for the grapevines are all in blossom." Song of Solomon 2:15

INTRODUCTION
Sandra grew up thinking that sex and love were synonymous. She thought that when a boy made her feel loved with gifts or dinner dates she was obliged to return his love by being physically intimate with him. She was seventeen when she spent her first summer away from home. Her aunt had promised that she could visit after graduation from high school. She met Austin at church where her aunt attended, and he offered to take her to a Six Flags theme park.

She accepted and was surprised that he only squeezed her hand when he took her home and said good night. They became friends. At the end of four weeks they returned to their first venue for their final date.

Sandra convinced herself that she was in love with him and wanted him to know that. As the day wore on she got physical. She put her arm around his neck and held his arm around her waist when they walked. She kissed him on the lips when they waited in line for rides. She even tried to sit on his lap as the attendant loaded the roller coaster.

Austin was surprised by this generous show of affection from a girl he had met only recently. He let her know that she was going too far.

"Well, don't you like me?" She was also surprised at his response.

"What does that have to do with all this crazy behavior?"

She explained about the type of dates she was accustomed to and how they usually ended. She assured him that she only wanted to return his affection. He informed her about his intention to walk pure.

Sandra's physical passion ruined her friendship with Austin. It made him uncomfortable. He knew that she was offering temptation that he did not need because it meant struggling to keep his passion in check.

Passion is only one of those sly foxes that we will deal with in this chapter. It feels good, but it can ruin a good friendship if not controlled by a pure mind. Thank God there are still men who commit to controlling their passion, hoping to meet and marry young women like you who commit to controlling yours.

There are so many areas in which you can invest your passion and have fun. Get excited about talents and skills that you share. Do profitable research together online. Compose lyrics and music for the song that will become "our song." Work together at community projects. Concentrate on building a pure and happy relationship.

In this chapter we will identify and deal with five tricky areas. They can contribute to a happy love relationship if they are filtered through the purity principle. If not, they can subtly pull your relationship into danger. They even begin with the same letter as purity:

(1) Passion
(2) Popularity
(3) Pity
(4) Pride
(5) Promises

1. Passion

a) Passion is defined as a strong feeling or emotion or an intense desire. How can you maintain a pure mind that makes the right decision with regard to passion? Romans 8:6

_____

_____

_____

_____

It is exciting to discover that a young man has affection for you; it is more exciting when your mind and body respond to his affection. His presence sends an electric surge up and down your spine. His voice puts fluttering butterflies into your stomach. You feel charged with extra energy, and you wonder what new thrills would come with embracing him.

The hormones released into your body beginning at puberty affect your thoughts and your emotions. When you fall in love you fantasize about physical closeness. You are tempted to abandon yourself to your desire for intimacy. Your feelings are normal and you have to get used to them. They remind you that you are alive and that it is your choice to control or abuse them.

You want to reserve your passion for that special moment with that special person whom you will marry. Even though you think you love that teenager, it is likely that you would be separated and lead different lives before you are both ready to settle down. If it turns out that you marry your high school sweetheart, the waiting will only affirm to each other how honorable you are.

b) What attribute of God helps you control your passion? What three terms, also meaning purity, are used to describe the life that accepts this gift from God? Titus 2:11, 12

_____

_____

_____

_____

The grace of God that saves you from your sins is the same grace that offers you the ability to control your passion. In the same way that you accept salvation willingly, be willing to accept the power of self-control.

2. Popularity

a) What physical assets made an Old Testament young woman popular? What did her popularity help her to achieve? Esther 2:7, 15, 17

_____

_____

_____

_____

Good looks are a blessing. They attract people to you, and it is your responsibility to show that your commitment to purity will not be compromised by your desire for popularity. Queen Vashti, who was replaced by Esther, was also beautiful, but when she refused to become a showpiece, she lost favor and popularity (Esther 1).

The man who is committed to purity wants his woman to please him, not the crowd. The woman who is committed to purity lives to please God first.

b) What action made Esther's popularity last? Esther 4:15, 16

_____

_____

_____

_____

_____

Physical beauty brought Esther to the throne, but beauty of character made her fulfill her purpose. Everyone has the need to belong, and that is healthy because we were made for interaction with family and friends. However, it is more important to pursue your purpose and accomplish your goals than to have people like you. People are fickle. They like you when you please them and dislike you when you don't. Standing for your personal convictions will always be attractive in a young woman.

3. Pity

a) To what lengths did an Old Testament man go in order to become intimate with a young woman? How does this incident prepare you to deal with young men who use sickness, heartache, loneliness, or any other situation to get close to you? 2 Samuel 13:7–14

_____

_____

_____

_____

Good girls are full of compassion. It is developed in the process of godly womanhood. Learn to be discreet and to offer help without becoming emotionally attached. Episodes like this make the Purity Circle seem necessary. When you are tempted to overspend time and energy in a relationship, a friend will warn you to consider your own safety and dignity.

b) What is more important than the nice things people think and say about you? Proverbs 31:30

_____

_____

_____

_____

It may seem heartless to someone who sees you turn down the opportunity to do a good deed. God knows when your motive is to avoid danger, and His reward is worth more to you than the praise of men.

4. Pride

a) What can young women take pride in knowing? Who is the source of the assets that you are proud of? Genesis 1:27; Psalms 139:14

_____

_____

_____

_____

Like all the foxes mentioned, pride works to your disadvantage when it is in excess. When it goes beyond, "I like who I am, because God made me," to "My assets, physical or otherwise, make me superior to someone else," it translates into self-conceit, arrogance, and vanity. That is when it becomes dangerous and tempts you to prove your fake superiority by any means.

However, in some young women it is the lack of pride that brings them down. Many young girls become self-conscious beginning with the discomfort and unpleasant experiences of menarche (the first menstrual period). They continue to feel worthless and unattractive through their young adult years. If you subscribe to this feeling of inferiority, you can become a target for garden intruders who promise to make you feel better.

Your female physiological differences are all part of a God-ordained process to present you to the opposite sex as an exceptional and mysterious piece of His work. Embrace your complexity; don't struggle with it. Low self-esteem is an invitation for callous men to prey on you. You are fearfully and wonderfully made. Conduct yourself with pride and dignity.

b) What did the young woman in the *Song* apologize for? If you were a member of her Purity Circle, how would you advise her? Song of Solomon 1:5, 6

_____

_____

_____

_____

c) What attribute of Jesus helps the young woman to keep her pride in a godly balance? How do you apply this in your own life? Matthew 11:29

_____

_____

_____

_____

_____

Godly pride makes you feel self-confident and worthy. It is different from vanity which makes you feel that you are better than someone else. Godly pride makes you consider that everybody is equally important to God.

5. Promises

a) What advice discourages young women from being gullible? Job 12:11

_____

_____

_____

_____

Promises! Promises! These little foxes come out in the open. Friends speak them to each other as evidence that the relationship has a good future. Pay attention and make sure that you understand them because it is easy for you to think that you hear what you want to hear. Also test them to see whether they are in keeping with the purity principle. For example, does he promise to be loyal if you do something immoral?

b) What advice is worth remembering when giving or receiving promises? Proverbs 12:22

_____

_____

_____

_____

Mandy became friends with a young man who convinced her that he loved her and wanted to commit to a serious relationship but that they had to keep their friendship a secret. He said that his culture did not allow him to date without his father's permission. He could not visit her house either until his father, who lived in another country, gave his blessing.

Mandy accepted his friendship, but she was uncomfortable with keeping it a secret. She began to doubt all that he had said about himself and his family. Still, she was willing to wait for his father's blessing, but he was unwilling to wait for physical intimacy. This suggested uneven exchange ended the relationship.

Your promise to remain pure underlies every other promise that you make. Keep the promise you made to God and trust Him to guide you into the acceptance or rejection of any promises which your friends make.

c) What promise has God made to you? How does this affect the promises you make and receive? 2 Timothy 2:21

_____

_____

_____

_____

POINTS TO REMEMBER

a) When the purity principle is in place, passion, popularity, pity, pride, and promises are all assets in the love relationship.
b) The mind that is controlled by God's Spirit is a mind that controls passion.
c) It is important to pursue your purpose in the midst of your popularity.
d) Uphold your safety and dignity in the midst of your compassion for others.
e) Walk with pride because of who you are and give God the glory.
f) The promises you give and accept reflect your commitment to purity.

Chapter 8

KNOW WHEN TO RUN

OBJECTIVES
(1)To help you discern abusive trends within your male-female relationships.
(2)To empower you to run away for your own safety.

THEME TEXT
"Run from anything that stimulates youthful lust. Follow anything that makes you want to do right. Pursue faith and love and peace, and enjoy the companionship of those who call on the Lord with pure hearts." 2 Timothy 2:22

INTRODUCTION
The following words are listed as by-products of "lust" in the Bible commentaries: covetousness, incest, homosexuality, vulgarity, profanity, and lewdness—the desire to excite sexual desires in an offensive way. Lust is a contributing factor to the abuse that some teens dish out when their partners do not cooperate in filling their wild desires. Often the abusers try to satisfy their lust through various forms of manipulation.

The advice is to run—move away quickly. This means that you do not have time to reason with the abuser or to wait for him to change. Remember that you can be compassionate without exposing yourself to danger. You can help more effectively if you move away and make space for someone who is qualified to diagnose and treat the abuser's problem.

Sara was fourteen and quite petite when she became friends with Don who was nineteen and seemed twice her size. She tried hard to prove her maturity, but Don never let her forget that she was just a kid. On a hot summer day she showed up at school wearing a turtleneck top with long sleeves.

In the classroom her best friend, Kim, leaned over toward her desk and laughed. "Did you watch a winter rerun on the weather channel this morning?"

Sara forced a smile but did not speak. Throughout the day other girls commented on her long sleeves, but she never laughed and she never spoke.

The turtleneck and the long sleeves appeared again on the following day. Kim wondered whether it was a laundry problem. "Tell me seriously, Sara," she said in a whisper, "Are all your summer tops in the wash? What's going on?"

Sara could tell that she cared and she promised to talk with her after school. As they walked towards the pick up area to wait for their rides, Don drove up tooting his horn.

"Ask him to wait," Kim suggested.

"I have to go," replied Sara as she started to run toward the car.

On Kim's persistence the next day, Sara told her story inside the girls' restroom. It was more like a show and tell.

Sara unbuttoned her shirt and showed Kim some blotches just below her neckline. There were bruises on both arms, and though Kim had not noticed, Sara had been holding her right ear occasionally because it pained her. Don had picked her up to go to his friend's house so they could make out. He lost his temper when she refused to go.

As she walked away, he followed her through her garage, held both her arms real firm from behind, and pushed her several times toward the wall. He hit her once on her ear as she turned her face to avoid bruising it on the wall.

She was ashamed to tell her parents because she did not want to hear them say, "We told you so." Only four weeks ago she had fought with them intensely for Don's right to visit her at home. She and Don had loud arguments before, but this was the first time he hit her.

"It was my fault," she told Kim. "I should have gone with him."

Kim was surprised to hear Sara say that. Was Sara so afraid of Don that she would give in to his lust and set herself up for further abuse?

This chapter looks at some ways in which young people abuse their friends and is a warning to take the signs seriously. Women as well as men are known to be abuse offenders. Some women also have the desire and the ability to manipulate their friends; women are not always the victims. The very best situation is to avoid abusive relationships completely, but for those who are already involved, it is never too late to run from:

(1) Physical abuse

(2) Verbal, mental, and emotional abuse

(3) Sexual abuse

DISCUSSION

1. Physical abuse

a) What physical image does the Bible give concerning the relationship of all believers? How would abuse from one person affect other believers? How would it affect Christ? Ephesians 2:20, 21 (See also 1 Corinthians 6:19, 20)

_____

_____

_____

See yourself as a beautiful piece of God's holy creation. Then realize that the God who made you also made the other person. In that frame of mind, none of the following forms of behavior would seem appropriate: hitting, pulling, pushing, punching, pinching, grabbing, slapping, shoving, kicking, twisting arms, boxing in corners, choking, or locking in cars or rooms. Abuse in any form stems from the abuser's desire to control the other person. God is the only supreme authority on your life. He created man and woman to dominate the earth together, not to dominate each other.

If your partner insists on manipulating you, put distance between you and him and encourage him to seek counseling help. If you find yourself initiating such abuse, seek help for yourself. Your Purity Circle group may be able to recommend counselors within your church or furnish phone numbers of hotlines and crime prevention agencies.

b) What substance usually causes someone to act violently? Proverbs 20:1

_____

_____

_____

_____

People under the influence of alcohol, marijuana, crack cocaine, heroin, and other street drugs, lose self-control and the ability to reason. Anger and bad tempers are dangerous by themselves, and intoxication makes the users even more violent. The U.S. Department of Justice reports that women between the ages of 16-24 experience the highest per capita rates of intimate violence, and that forty percent of young women between the ages of 14-17 say they know someone who has been physically abused by a boyfriend. No wonder the theme text advises that you choose friends who believe in the purity lifestyle.

2. Verbal, mental, and emotional abuse
Words are used in all these forms of abuse, and they are all related.

a) What is the purity guideline for conversation? Proverbs 4:24; Ephesians 5:4

_____

_____

_____

_____

That rules out all forms of verbal abuse: name-calling, criticism, belittling, mocking, negative comparisons to others, and any joke about women being stupid or worthless. Abusers intend to control their victims by inflicting mental anguish and emotional pain. They try to make their victims feel guilty, embarrassed, worthless, and humiliated. Some of their non-verbal tactics, include spending time with other people to make their victims feel jealous, or ignoring them when they want to talk. Some victims become accustomed to the abuse and accept it as a regular part of the relationship. This is very dangerous because it takes much effort to change such faulty thinking.

At the first sign that your friend is a control freak, you need to run. Some of the signs will be listed in the chapter summary.

b) How can you tell the difference between verbal abuse and verbal empowerment? Proverbs 12:6, 18, 25, 26

_____

_____

_____

_____

When other people's words about you do not comply with the social posture you created for yourself, recognize the lies and dismiss them. Keep company with friends whose words affirm you and give you good counsel.

3. Sexual abuse

a) What are the reasons given for running away from sexual sins? 1 Corinthians 6:18

_____

_____

_____

_____

Some young people ignore the warning to run from sexual sins. Instead they try to see how close they can get without engaging in sex. They kiss, they explore each other's bodies, and they lock themselves in each other's embrace trying to satisfy their physical urges. Lately, it has been reported that young girls have been serving up satisfaction to their boyfriends through oral sex which they think is an appropriate parting kiss. Satisfying sexual urges is moving slowly but surely towards the sex act, not at all running from it. Please refuse to do it, and if you are being forced to do it, consider yourself sexually abused.

Sexual abuse includes pressuring someone into the act, through guilt trips and threats of ending the relationship. Inappropriate touching, comments about breasts, buttocks, thighs, and any other form of unwanted advances are considered sexual harassment. Unwanted phone calls, e-mails, or notes should be reported. Introducing pornographic material is also abuse.

There are many attempts being made on the internet to lure young women into sexual escapades. Be careful to avoid websites that offer sexual content.

(b) What form of sexual abuse happened between Amnon and Tamar whose story we looked at in the last chapter? 2 Samuel 13:14 How would you suggest that Tamar deals with it if Amnon asked her to keep it a secret?

_____

_____

_____

_____

Bad things happen to good people no matter how many precautions they take. If you ever suffer any form of abuse, do not let shame or guilt control your life. A large number of rapes by family members and boyfriends go unreported because the victim feels that she will be blamed for causing a disruption to the offender's life, or because no one will believe her report. This is unfortunate, and I pray that it never happens to any member of the Purity Circle. However, in the event that it does, do yourself a favor, and talk about it. Get the support of peers or trustworthy adults and make a report. It is never your fault that you are a victim. Deal with it so that you can recover from the emotional hurt and return to being the woman that God had in mind when He made you.

c) When you run from abuse and you still get hurt, to whom do you run then? What can you hope for? Psalms 34:17, 18

_____

_____

_____

_____

Thank God for sending Jesus to save us not only from sin, but also from the damaging effects of it. You can be healed and enjoy full physical, mental, and emotional health again. Get help! Hang out with your friends who are godly, and enjoy the happy youth and young adult years that you deserve. Be careful and prayerful!

POINTS TO REMEMBER

a) God is the only authority on your life; resist the control of anyone else.

b) Refuse to keep company with anyone who uses alcohol or street drugs.

c) Abuse is never the fault of the victim.

d) Do not keep abuse secret; ask your Purity Circle for help to deal with it.

e) Run from relationships in which a man of any age exhibits any characteristics of an abuser:

    i. Monitors your activities and phone calls, as if he owns you

    ii. Wants to make all your decisions for you

    iii. Displays excessive jealousy when you talk with other friends

    iv. Exhibits bad temper, mood swings, and looses control

    v. Calls you names and embarrasses you in public

    vi. Intimidates you so you feel afraid when you are with him

    vii. Asks you to keep secrets.

f) Run to God for healing and restoration after any form of abuse. If it is your friend who is abused, help her find healing.

Chapter 9

GIRLFRIENDS

OBJECTIVE

To present guidelines that will help you build long-term female friendships.

THEME TEXT

"Don't think only about your own affairs, but be interested in others, too, and what they are doing." Philippians 2:4

INTRODUCTION

My teenage son was friendly with all four girls in the clique, and any one of them would have accepted his invitation to be his date for the banquet. When he selected one, I assumed that the others would be upset.

To my surprise, when I drove him to the house to pick up the chosen one, the other three girls were at her house seated around like ladies-in-waiting.

"What is everybody doing here?" I said wondering if they had some trick up their sleeves.

"I came over to fix her hair," offered the first.

"We helped her choose her dress. We just want to make sure…"

"That she looks her best," the third one finished.

It was a beautiful picture—girls working together to present friendship at its best. Three of them shared in the happy experience of their friend, knowing that each of them could look forward to the same support when future opportunities presented themselves. Attitudes like this force young men to admire and respect female bonds. They think twice before trying to deceive girlfriends by playing them against each other.

In the *Song,* the young woman asks her friends to help her when her lover is absent, and they offer to help her find him (Song of Solomon 6:1). Like them, it is your Christian duty to take a healthy interest in your sister's business, not to control it, but to support it.

Girlfriends love each other and want to see each other succeed. They bond closely together to protect themselves from hostile forces outside the circle. Finding boyfriends is not their only interest. They also want to see themselves progress together in spiritual and educational matters. Later, they become interested in achieving their economic goals.

It is not unusual for high school friendships to last through college and survive time and distance through adulthood. These are precious friendships, filled with the memories that will energize you in the midst of the stresses that come with adulthood. This is the time to pack your friendships with the fun and laughter that you will recall twenty and thirty years from now.

There are some challenges that come with lifetime friendships, but you can overcome them and survive together. The rewards outweigh the challenges. Friends nurture each other by sharing the following benefits of friendship:

(1) Affirmation—talk about the good qualities in each other.

(2) Advice—counsel on what is right, wrong, appropriate, etc.

(3) Assistance—help with your individual projects.

(4) Accountability—requiring that you explain your decisions and actions.

(5) Applause—cheers and praise when you make strides and perform at your personal best.

DISCUSSION

1. Affirmation

a) What godly counsel makes a good motto for girlfriends in the Purity Circle? 1 Thessalonians 5:11

_____

_____

_____

_____

Notice the good traits in each other. Compliment each other on humor, kindness, friendliness, taste in dress, and any other quality that you admire. If you make it a habit to affirm the good in each other, selfishness and jealousy will not have space to grow. Because God designed a special purpose for each one, He designed each character with different strengths. Appreciate your virtues, and let your friends know that you admire theirs.

Jealousy among girlfriends surfaces occasionally. Their jealousy is not necessarily hateful. For example, if you and your friend like the same young man and your friend gains his attention, you may say, "I wish he had chosen me, but although he picked her, I want them to be happy because she is my friend."

You and your girlfriend still need the support of your friendship. You both still have the virtues you admired in each other before the man entered the picture. Keep on affirming and strengthening each other. The males who befriend you will learn to be respectful and supportive too.

b) What is the flip side of affirmation, and why should you be careful to avoid it? Proverbs 26:28

_____

_____

_____

_____

The purity principle promotes honesty in speech. If you are ever tempted to lie in an attempt to make your friends feel good, take an extra minute to think of something true. Trust is important in friendship, and it begins with the confidence to trust each other's word. That makes it easy to choose between what they hear from you and what they hear from their special male friend.

c) Share some affirmation now. Write affirmations for three people in the group. The group leader will tell you how to select your three so that everyone gets selected.

_____

_____

_____

_____

Do this often in your meetings, and even at other times when your friends least expect it. Let the Purity Circle be a source of inspiration and validation for all the members.

NOTE: Affirmation also includes validation—accepting what someone says about herself. For example, your friend may say that she is scared, feels guilty, or is being abused. You may not understand her reasons for her feelings and may doubt that she is telling the truth. Do not judge her according to your opinion. Try to put her at ease by telling her that she has a right to her emotion. If she needs help that you cannot give, ask her permission to enlist someone else.

2. Assistance

a) What is your responsibility to your friends who are committed to godly living? List some ways in which members of your Purity Circle might need your help. Galatians 6:10

_____

_____

_____

_____

b) What is the underlying motive of Christian friends who help each other? 1 Peter 4:11

_____

_____

_____

_____

The joy in helping comes from the satisfaction that you did something pleasing to God, not from having everyone know what help you gave and to whom. Your friends appreciate your help, and if you are patient as well as kind, you will hear them affirm your kindness even if not immediately.

3. Advice

a) How does good friendly advice affect the friend who is receiving the advice? Proverbs 27:9

_____

_____

_____

_____

People accept advice more readily from friends who also affirm them. It is not friendly to only point out the bad. Advice is pleasant like perfume when it comes from a friend who cares.

Friends give advice on personal matters like male-female relationships, misunderstanding with parents, appropriate dress, and music. It is helpful to have friends who understand your concerns and make time to talk with you. Cherish their input, weigh their counsel, but remember that the final decision is yours.

b) What does the wise man think about receiving counsel from more than one person? Proverbs 11:14

_____

_____

_____

_____

Sometimes to avoid counsel, young people are tempted to be secretive. There is never a good reason to hide the facts about your relationship with a male from your girlfriends. Better to bring it out in the open and get advice early.

4. Accountability

a) In the Song of Solomon, what question do the young woman's friends ask her? Song of Solomon 5:8, 9 Do you think that they have a right to know?

_____

_____

_____

_____

They were listening to her dream about this young man, and they asked her to explain her interest in him. Real friends will ask you questions like this, because they want to help you figure out if the young man deserves your attention and if you are proceeding in the right direction. Often when you explain yourself to your friends, they ask more questions that make you think more clearly. You are more careful about your decisions and actions when you know that your friends will ask questions.

b) Who else besides your friends requires your accountability? Romans 14:12

_____

_____

_____

_____

If you feel comfortable about the answers you give to your friends, it is likely that you will be able to talk to God with a clear conscience. When you talk with your friends, remember that God knows even the information that you do not give to them. Be honest with your friends; they help you to be honest with yourself and with God.

5. Applause

a) What event caused the children of Israel to cheer for King David? Who led the cheer? 1 Samuel 18:6

_____

_____

_____

_____

A victory deserves a celebration, and women make good cheerleaders. You boost your friend's self-worth when you notice her achievements and call other people's attention to it. It also makes you feel encouraged because you realize that you also can experience victory, if even in a different skill. Celebration among friends adds to your archive of pleasant memories.

b) What is unfortunate about the way King Saul reacted to the applause? 1 Samuel 18:7–9

_____

_____

_____

_____

Applause is another reason that friends may become jealous of each other when some receive more than others. Sometimes your friends do not even realize that you are hurt. Discuss your feelings rather than let your jealousy turn to anger. The wise man says that, "Wounds from a friend are better than many kisses from an enemy" (Proverbs 27:6). That is because friends do not mean to hurt you, and they will do something to change the negative situation; enemies may have ulterior motives even when their actions seem right.

To ensure that every friend in your circle receives adequate attention, select each one for her turn to receive affirmation and applause. Choose a different friend at each meeting, or during her birth month, or draw names from a hat.

c) Write or copy a friendship poem expressing your love and support for a friend. Write it without knowing which member of your group will receive it. Your commitment to each one is the same, anyway. Decide on a time when you will exchange poems. Have fun and begin a collection of friendship keepsakes!

_____
_____
_____
_____
_____
_____
_____
_____
_____
_____
_____
_____
_____
_____
_____
_____
_____

POINTS TO REMEMBER

a) Youth is the time to make memories that you want to remember in adulthood.
b) Friends build each other's self–esteem with affirmation.
c) Assistance to friends is also service to God.
d) Don't be secretive about your male friends just to avoid the advice of your female friends.
e) Answering your friends honestly helps you to be honest with God.
f) Celebrating your friend's victory encourages you to expect your own success.

Chapter 10

LITTLE SISTERS

OBJECTIVES

(1)To show the importance of spiritual and moral growth.
(2)To teach tolerance for those who develop slowly.

THEME TEXT

"We have a little sister too young for breasts. What will we do if someone asks to marry her? If she is chaste, we will strengthen her and encourage her. But if she is promiscuous, we will shut her off from men." Song of Solomon 8:8, 9

INTRODUCTION

Breasts are the metaphor for womanhood, so the young woman in our text has not developed the skills and graces of womanhood. No one expects a young woman's breasts to be fully developed, but how do you think she feels with no breasts at all?

Her Purity Circle asks, "What will we do?" She needs help from friends who will not turn their backs on her when her weakness shows. The way they deal with her depends on whether she is chaste or promiscuous, according to the text.

Here is a dialogue between a young woman and the man with whom she has a relationship. See if you could determine in which group she belongs.

Delilah: You have been making fun of me and telling me lies! Won't you please tell me how you can be tied up securely?

Samson: If you weave the seven braids of my hair into the fabric on your loom and tighten it with the loom shuttle, I will be as weak as anyone else.

(So while he slept, Delilah wove the seven braids of his hair into the fabric and tightened it with the loom shuttle.)

Delilah: Samson! The Philistines have come to capture you!

(Samson woke up, pulled back the loom shuttle, and yanked his hair away from the loom and the fabric.)

Delilah (pouting): How can you say you love me when you don't confide in me? You've made fun of me three times now, and you still haven't told me what makes you so strong!

(So day after day she nagged him until he couldn't stand it any longer.)

Samson: My hair has never been cut for I was dedicated to God as a Nazirite from birth. If my head were shaved my strength would leave me, and I would become as weak as anyone else.

Delilah (to the Philistine leaders): Come back one more time for he has told me everything.

(The Philistine leaders returned and brought money with them. Delilah lulled Samson to sleep with his head in her lap, and she called in a man to shave off his hair, making his capture certain.)

Delilah: Samson! The Philistines have come to capture you!

(So the Philistines captured him and gouged out his eyes. They took him to Gaza where he was bound with bronze chains and made to grind grain in the prison.) Judges 16:14–21

Delilah would be a challenge for her Purity Circle. She tells lies. She pretends to love Samson, but she deceives him in exchange for money and popularity.

She represents some young women who are already corrupt when you meet them. They are little sisters regardless of their physical ages, because figuratively, either they have no breasts or their breasts are underdeveloped. They need to learn godly womanhood.

This chapter puts little sisters into two groups and discusses the help they need:

(1)Chaste little sisters

(2)Promiscuous little sisters

DISCUSSION

1. Chaste little sisters

a) What kind of help does a chaste sister need? The King James Version calls her a wall. How is that comparison fitting for a chaste woman? Song of Solomon 8:9

_____

_____

_____

_____

Find her strengths and affirm her. Would a wall be more or less attractive with decorations? Women like to bring out the softer, nurturing qualities in each other.

b) What training helps the chaste young woman become a mature godly woman? Titus 2:4, 5

_____

_____

_____

_____

It is never too early for chaste young women to begin learning how to become godly adult women. Here are the five basic areas of training mentioned in the verses:

i) Love for husbands and children

At your age, you can begin to learn respect for men. Learn how to compliment, encourage, and express appreciation to your male friends. Practice appropriate behaviors when you are alone with your special friend and when both of you are in company with other people. Set boundaries for the attention you give to his friends and the attention they give to you. These habits will transfer to your role as wife, and your children will imitate you.

ii) Wisdom, self-control, and purity

Shirley lost her part-time job which provided the money to pay for her cell phone. She shared her dilemma with Robert, and he had a ready suggestion. "Come, hang out with us at the club this weekend," he told her, "and I'll get the boys to chip in."

Saturday night came. Shirley lied about going to the movies with two of her girl-friends, and all three of them went to the club. The others were drinking and took turns insisting that she take a sip.

"I won't drink enough to get drunk," she said to herself. "I'll take just one sip to please them."

"Keeping the phone was worth it," she thought. Then for one brief moment, an image of her standing drunk before her parents flashed in her mind. She did not want that to become a reality. The struggle to keep her phone or remain sober lasted for what seemed like hours. Finally, she made the right choice and asked her girl friends to take her home. Purity and self-control are developed by practice.

iii)Home management

Home management is a skill that could be rewarding and exciting if you are prepared for it. Study how to schedule your time so that as a homemaker you can create your own delicacies in the kitchen and still have time for shopping, beauty shop appointments, and concerts.

Learn now to control your spending and avoid the bondage of cell phone and credit card debt.

You will gain the reputation of the virtuous woman, "She carefully watches all that goes on in her household and does not have to bear the consequences of laziness." Proverbs 31:27

iv) Good deeds

Kindness and all its synonyms (compassion, caring, mercy, and hospitality) come naturally to the godly woman. It is a quality that attracts both male and female friends to you. They respond with cooperation and respect.

v) Submission

Submission is a beautiful concept to a young woman who understands it. Simply put, it is an attitude that allows both the man and the woman in a relationship to recognize and accept the support of each other. Learn to respect a man for who he is, and do not try to remake him or fix him. Only God can change a man.

Get him to respect you by respecting yourself. Be sincere in the contributions you make to the relationship. You do not have to become a superwoman and compare yourself with him. Be a supporter not a controller.

c) What is the difference between a little sister and a mature sister? How does the training pay off? Song of Solomon 8:10

_____

_____

_____

_____

A young woman becomes a mature sister for her own satisfaction, for the happiness of her future mate, and for the glory of God.

2. Promiscuous sisters

a) What kind of help does a promiscuous sister need? The King James Version calls her a door. How is that comparison fitting for a promiscuous sister? Song of Solomon 8:9

_____

_____

_____

_____

A young woman who continually goes in and out of sexual relationships is like a door that swings in and out. So the first step is to close the door and keep the men out. Young women in the Purity Circle need the help of an adult counselor who understands the struggles of the promiscuous sister. Meanwhile, your attitude toward her can help her feel that she is in the company of friends who care.

b) What advice is appropriate for the promiscuous little sister? Romans 6:12, 13

_____

_____

_____

_____

When a young woman abuses her body in premarital sex, with one or more partners, she exposes herself to unwanted physical consequences. Pregnancies and STDs have long term effects with long term regrets. However, even if she manages to avoid pregnancy and disease, promiscuity would still be disastrous.

Premarital sex also has mental and emotional consequences. It destroys self-esteem, making the young woman feel cheap and unworthy of real love from an honorable man.

Young women become emotionally attached to their sexual partners and find it difficult to break the emotional bond after the partners neglect them and move on. They feel torn and every new partner leaves them feeling less whole. They continue to surrender their bodies hoping to find the love that continues to elude them. The friendship and counsel of concerned loyal sisters can offer the emotional support to curb this destructive behavior.

c) What attitude on her part will help her change her conduct? What attitude on your part will help her? Romans 6:19; Colossians 3:12–14

_____

_____

_____

_____

The following parable was written to encourage a little sister who became pregnant. The principles of restoration and forgiveness apply to any young woman who repents from immoral conduct and accepts God's forgiveness.

The Parable of the Wedding Gown

I am a bridal gown designed for that special young woman who, from her earliest days of bows and frills, has dreamed of adorning her beauty within a style like mine.

I come with matching veil and shoes. My wearer will select her favorite accessory, and assemble her choicest bouquet to complete her attire for her most memorable occasion. Yet, of all the fashionable items on display that day, I will be the center of attention.

Some will look at me more intensely than they look at the face of the bride, for they will discuss me afterwards with those who did not see me. Photographers will snap at me from every angle, and when they develop the films, the prints will be accepted or rejected according to the way I turn out.

Since everyone thinks so much of me, it is only fair that I relate my story.

Just yesterday, I was hanging tall with other gowns upon a rack. The push and pull of anxious brides-to-be had been sliding me closer and closer to the edge, but nobody noticed. One woman barely touched me as she walked by, and I fell onto the floor. The sales clerk rushed to my rescue, quickly dusted me, and hung me back in place, but not fast enough to prevent my neighbor gown from noticing

When I settled on the rack again, my neighbor offered, "They'll have to mark you down. No one will pay full price for a gown that once lay on the floor."

"What an awful shame!" I sobbed. "Falling to the ground is a major tragedy in the life of a wedding gown."

Just then the manager came over to the sales clerk. She spoke some words that sounded to me as melodious as the wedding march sounds to the bride on her wedding day.

"This gown fell," she said, "but it did not remain on the ground, and it wasn't crushed. You thoroughly dusted it and put it back on the rack. It has resumed its original shape. This gown is worth the full price because the fall did not change the fact that a prestigious manufacturer designed it with materials of the richest quality. A temporary fall cannot alter the worth of so valuable a gown."

You should have seen my fabric glow. My faith and hope rekindled. So now I want to share my sense of worth with the young woman who will select me for her special day.

You too may have fallen from the rack of virtuous womanhood. Women stain faster and deeper than gowns do, but the One who rushes to your rescue is the most competent at restoration. He can put you back on the full price rack, if you will let Him. He invested His most valuable product—His life—in you, and your worth can never be discounted. Your fall gives you added responsibility (and He will help you carry it), but it does not mark you down.

Please wear me with pride. And as your guests admire you and me, do outshine me with a smile of confidence, for you have the much greater worth.

POINTS TO REMEMBER

a) It is never too early to begin learning the basics of godly womanhood.
b) Be tolerant with those who learn slowly.
c) The basics of womanhood include respect for men.
d) Even without pregnancies and STDs, premarital sex is still destructive.
e) Purity and self-control are developed by practice.
f) God forgives and restores young women who repent from their immorality.

Chapter 11

CELEBRATING THE PURITY CIRCLE

OBJECTIVE

To consider the eternal value of the purity lifestyle and the friendship circle

THEME TEXT

"Now to Him who is able to protect you from stumbling and to make you stand in the presence of His glory, blameless and with great joy." Jude 1:24

INTRODUCTION

The Kingdom of Heaven can be illustrated by the story of ten high school young women who formed a Purity Circle and decided to help each other "live wisely and be pure." (Titus 2:5) Five of them were new to the purity lifestyle, and five of them grew up practicing it.

The five who were new enjoyed the friendship of the others, but did not have the courage to say with certainty that they would "walk pure." The other five were wise enough to commit to the purity pledge. During the years they spent together, the experienced five lived the purity principle while their friends watched, learned, and accepted the challenge.

On graduation from high school, they were greeted by the challenge, "Don't let any-one think less of you because you are young. Be an example to all believers in what you teach, in the way you live, in your love, faith, and your purity." (1 Timothy 4:12)

All the young women braced themselves and looked forward to their adventure in college. Then the five who learned from their friends said to the five who taught them, "Thank you for teaching us about the purity lifestyle. Now give us some of your courage to help us stand firm when we go off to our different colleges, and we face temptation alone."

The five who were experienced replied, "You will never truly be alone. Christ stands by you as He stands by us, and He is faithful. 'He will keep the temptation from becoming so strong that you can't stand up against it. When you are tempted, he will show you a way out so that you will not give in to it.'" (1 Corinthians 10:13)

"We will also keep in touch to affirm each other, advise each other, and be ac-countable to each other. We remain friends helping friends live pure."

While the young women went their different ways, their friendships continued and the purity lifestyle remained their focus.

When they faced the challenges of final exams, meeting new friends, and making decisions, they shared moral support. They rejoiced as each one reported strides in personal progress and relationships.

When the first young woman got married, all her bridesmaids were from her Purity Circle. Beauty and purity shone through all ten. No one could tell the difference between the five who practiced purity all their lives, and the five who learned it later.

On the wedding night, the groom said to his bride, "You are so beautiful, my beloved, so perfect in every part....You are like a private garden, my treasure, my bride! You are like a spring that no one else can drink from, a fountain of my own. You are like a lovely orchard bearing precious fruit, with the rarest of perfumes." (Song of Solomon 4:7, 12, 13)

And she thought, "So are all my friends. We're all beautiful and pure and Jesus will say the same about us when He presents us to His Father, 'For they are spiritually undefiled, pure as virgins, following the Lamb wherever He goes.'" (Revelation 14:4)

"So, be careful how you live, not as fools but as those who are wise." (Ephesians 5:15, 17)

This chapter examines the parable of the ten virgins (Matthew 25:1–13) who had different results from the members of the Purity Circle described above. They were ten women preparing for the greatest event of their lives. Five were naive about what they needed to do, while five were fully prepared and were successful. There are two issues to look at:

(1) Understanding the goal
(2) Team effort versus individual effort

DISCUSSION

1. Understanding the goal

a) What was the common goal of the ten virgins? How does their goal compare with the goal of the Purity Circle? Matthew 25:1, Jude 1:24

_____

_____

_____

_____

Your long-term goal is to have Jesus present you pure and whole to His heavenly Father as a citizen of Heaven. All your other goals for education, career, marriage, and family are steps toward meeting your final goal.

b) What responsibility did each one have, in order to meet their goal? How does that compare with the individual responsibility of each Purity Circle member? Matthew 25:8, 9

_____

_____

_____

_____

Each young woman is responsible for her own personal relationship with God. It is her daily duty to surrender her heart, her mind, and her body to Jesus and allow the Holy Spirit to guide her in her purity walk.

The goal is not to sit still while your friends make decisions for you and tell you what to do. They can advise you and assist you, but they cannot make you live a pure life. They can teach you nutrition and personal body care, but they will not put the right food in your mouth and they will not dress you. They will not prevent you from getting drunk if you choose to drink alcohol. They will not prevent you from having sex if you take your boyfriend into your bedroom. The Purity Circle will give you moral support when you choose to do what is right.

2. Team effort versus individual effort

a) What secondary goal did Paul have for the church groups? How does that goal help the Purity Circle to achieve its primary goal? Colossians 2:2

_____

_____

_____

_____

Being a member of the Purity Circle means more than wanting the purity lifestyle for yourself. It means that you are connected with the other members of the circle, and that you are interested in seeing them succeed. Even though you cannot force someone to pull her weight, you can encourage her as much as you can because she is your sister. Don't give-up on anyone.

b) How can you tell that the virgins did not work as a team? How could things have turned out differently if they practiced the Purity Circle concept of sisterhood? Matthew 25:5–10

_____

_____

_____

_____

In your Purity Circle, you have the opportunity to see the weaknesses of each other. When you offer advice and assistance, remember that your aim is preparation for adulthood, and for heaven. Friends want friends to enjoy this life now and eternal life afterwards.

c) Can you write from memory the motto in 1 Thessalonians 5:11? How does that verse compare with Matthew 25:13?

_____

_____

_____

_____

d) What benefits have you already gained from being in the Purity Circle? Add to your list as you continue enjoying the circle of *friends helping friends live pure*.

_____

_____

_____

_____

POINTS TO REMEMBER
a) The parable of the Ten Virgins teaches us not to live foolishly, but wisely.
b) Each young woman is responsible for her purity walk.
c) Purity Circle members are interested in helping each other succeed.
d) Even when distant from each other, Purity Circle members support each other by prayers and other encouraging gestures.
e) Purity Circle members look forward to presenting themselves pure and whole to their future spouses on earth, and to their Lord and Master in heaven.
f) Heaven is the final goal of the Purity Circle.

THE FINALE

The climax of Christ's work on earth is His return for those who will share eternal life with Him. This is Heaven's Olympic moment—the single most glorious event in time and in eternity.

He could choose any of His creative handiwork as metaphors for the descent of the Holy City, the New Jerusalem, coming down to receive His people. He could choose the sunrise to describe its mysterious and colorful approach; He could choose the ocean deep and wide to compare with the vastness of its space; He could choose the lily to depict its elegance and beauty; He could choose the stars to portray the dazzling permanence of its precious stones; He could choose the eagle, so majestic and powerful in its flight through the heavens, but none of these made His selection.

His preferred image to symbolize the most glorious event in our world is the picture of a completely pure woman—*His woman,* whom He takes to be His bride. (Revelation 21:9). That tells you that He thinks highly of women; that you are special to Him; that pleasing Him in your youth is the best thing you could possibly do.

Visualize the grandeur of the Holy City and the smiling face of Jesus welcoming the joyful saints who share His purity. See yourself among them. Look around for the other members of your Purity Circle. Now see other Purity Circles join with yours to become the great Purity Circle which Christ will present to His Father. What a glorious sight!

Purity is beauty and it lasts forever.

PURITY PRINCIPLES AND PROMISES

"How can a young person stay pure? By obeying your word and following its rules" (Psalms 119:9). However, in order to obey it you have to know it.

During the Purity Pledge Ceremony, each Purity Circle member will recite a Bible passage that you have chosen to memorize. You will adopt this verse or verses and keep them planted in your heart—to be used as your own personal energizer in your purity walk.

Below are two groups of verses, ten in each group, under the heading of Principles and Promises. You may choose one of the passages as your memory text, or you may select from the Bible any portion of Scripture that has personal meaning to you.

Whatever passage you choose, feel free to include it as often as necessary in your conversation with members of your Purity Circle. The more you speak it, the more it will empower you to live it.

PRINCIPLES

- "People judge by outward appearance, but the LORD looks at a person's thoughts and intentions." 1 Samuel 16:7
- "Do not let any part of your body become a tool of wickedness, to be used for sinning. Instead, give yourselves completely to God since you have been given new life. And use your whole body as a tool to do what is right for the glory of God." Romans 6:12, 13
- "Don't you know that your body is the temple of the Holy Spirit, who lives in you and was given to you by God? You do not belong to yourself, for God bought you with a high price. So you must honor God with your body." 1 Corinthians 6:19, 20
- "Let there be no sexual immorality, impurity, or greed among you. Such sins have no place among God's people. Obscene stories, foolish talk, and coarse jokes— these are not for you. Instead, let there be thankfulness to God." Ephesians 5:3, 4
- "So be careful how you live, not as fools but as those who are wise. Make the most of every opportunity for doing good in these evil days. Don't act thoughtlessly, but try to understand what the Lord wants you to do." Ephesians 5:15–17
- "Whatever is true, whatever is noble, whatever is right, whatever is pure, whatever is lovely, whatever is admirable—if anything is excellent or praiseworthy—think about such things." Philippians 4:8 (NIV)
- "And I want women to be modest in their appearance. They should wear decent and appropriate clothing and not draw attention to themselves by the way they

fix their hair or by wearing gold or pearls or expensive clothes. For women who claim to be devoted to God should make themselves attractive by the good things they do." 1 Timothy 2:9, 10

- "Run from anything that stimulates youthful lust. Follow anything that makes you want to do right. Pursue faith and love and peace, and enjoy the companionship of those who call on the Lord with pure hearts." 2 Timothy 2:22
- "Don't let anyone think less of you because you are young. Be an example to all believers in what you teach, in the way you live, in your love, your faith, and your purity." 1 Timothy 4:12
- "Don't be concerned about the outward beauty that depends on fancy hairstyles, expensive jewelry, or beautiful clothes. You should be known for the beauty that comes from within, the unfading beauty of a gentle and quiet spirit, which is so precious to God." 1 Peter 3:3, 4

PROMISES

- "To the faithful you show yourself faithful; to those with integrity you show integrity." 2 Samuel 2:26
- "The righteous will move onward and forward, and those with pure hearts will become stronger and stronger." Job 17:9
- "Who may climb the mountain of the LORD? Who may stand in his holy place? Only those whose hands and hearts are pure, who do not worship idols and never tell lies." Psalms 24:3, 4
- "Charm is deceptive, and beauty is fleeting; but a woman who fears the LORD is to be praised." Proverbs 31:30
- "God blesses those whose hearts are pure, for they will see God." Matthew 5:8
- "If your sinful nature controls your mind, there is death. But if the Holy Spirit controls your mind, there is life and peace." Romans 8:6
- "But remember that the temptations that come into your life are no different from what others experience. And God is faithful. He will keep the temptation from becoming so strong that you can't stand up against it. When you are tempted, he will show you a way out so that you will not give in to it." 1 Corinthians 10:13
- "If you keep yourself pure, you will be a utensil God can use for his purpose. Your life will be clean, and you will be ready for the Master to use you for every good work." 2 Timothy 2:21
- "But if we confess our sins to him, he is faithful and just to forgive us and to cleanse us from every wrong." 1 John 1:9
- "And now, all glory to God, who is able to keep you from stumbling, and who will bring you into his glorious presence innocent of sin and with great joy." Jude 1:24

To Purity Circle Members and Leaders

The Purity Circle founders would like to receive feedback concerning your circle's response to the workbook material. We would also like to hear about your activities.

Feel free to contact us with questions and suggestions at: PurityCircle@usa. com

PURITY CIRCLE WORKBOOK GUIDE

(for the Purity Circle Instructor)

CONTENTS

INTRODUCTION

Purity Circle attempts to help young women age ten and onward find the trail that leads to godly womanhood. It provides a forum in which they can learn the Biblical principles of purity. It teaches them to apply these principles as they struggle through the maze of immoral suggestions in the secular magazines, song lyrics, television programs, websites and other ungodly sources.

In addition to their primary decision to accept Jesus as their Lord and Master, the program emphasizes two other commitments:
(1) a commitment to a lifestyle of purity;
(2) a commitment to supporting their friends in the purity walk.

Purity Circle takes seriously the Biblical mandate, that "older women must train the younger women to...live wisely and be pure" (Titus 2:4, 5). Instructors should expect to find a variety of situations which offer an opportunity to continue the ministry of Jesus (Luke 4:18, 19): teaching those who desire to learn, healing those who are emotionally damaged, delivering those who are entrapped and abused, directing those who cannot find their way, offering salvation to those who desire to accept Jesus as their Savior.

The purity lifestyle is all encompassing and the purity instructor prepares for the task by daily personal commitment to Jesus who supplies the grace and strength for this assignment. No woman involved in teaching purity by precept and example can question the purpose for her life

Thanks for accepting the challenge. The young women will appreciate us and God will reward us.

INSTRUCTOR'S PRAYER

Once upon a Bible time, a woman went looking for Jesus to find healing for a young woman who was being tormented by an evil spirit. See Matthew 15:21–28. (Bear in mind that promiscuity, body piercing, obscenity, drug abuse, vulgarity, rudeness and all other forms of immorality are influenced by some spirit other than the Spirit of God.)

Although it was the young woman who needed help, the older woman's first prayer was for herself, "Lord help me" (15:22 NIV).

As instructors we cannot distance ourselves from the need for purity. We can only give to the young women what we ourselves have. The Bible woman's prayer is appropriate for us because:

(1) We need courage to accept and teach God's principles, not ours.
(2) We need strength to live up to the principles we teach.
(3) We need compassion to minister to the specific needs of each young woman.
(4) We need wisdom to deal with opposing influences.

(5) We need physical and spiritual energy to persevere for as long as it takes.

We may encounter difficulties from non-supportive parents or church folk who misunderstand our passion. Some young women may appear unreceptive. Sometimes we may even be tempted to think that God disregards our prayers on their behalf. At such times, like the woman in the Bible, it pays to keep on petitioning Him and insisting that we want each of our young women to have her share of His purity.

God wants to restore His purity principles in the hearts and lives of every young woman within our sphere of influence. He can use us to reach them. "Lord, help us."

THE PROGRAM

The Purity Circle program begins with eleven workbook sessions. We suggest that these sessions be held weekly, but each group can decide its own agenda.

The first five lessons lead up to the Purity Pledge Ceremony (See Page vii). The ceremony is the sixth session. There are five other lessons after the pledge. There is also an appendix of Bible verses from which each young woman may select one for recital in the pledge ceremony. They are not limited to these verses; they may choose any verse of scripture, including the theme text at the beginning of each chapter.

Instructors are encouraged to study each lesson before presenting it. Try to create a circle around a table on which they could place their workbook lessons and Bibles. An opening and closing prayer is appropriate, and all Bible verses should be read. Bibles should be provided for everyone. Encourage class discussion. Recognize and respond to each question.

Feel free to engage your creativity, including illustrations and personal experiences. However, try not to direct focus on your struggles instead of the young women's. Always present Christ as the source of their help. He supplies the principles for the purity walk. You are just a coach.

Do not be in a hurry to complete each lesson in one session. If it takes more than twelve weeks to complete the workbook, persevere. At the end of each session, if time permits, have each member state a purity idea that is meaningful to her. It is acceptable for them to repeat the *Points To Remember* listed at the end of each chapter.

Form other groups if the membership becomes more than fifteen. Encourage close friends to belong to the same group, so they can relate the lessons to their specific situations. It will be also meaningful for them to pledge together.

None of the lessons initiate discussion on masturbation, lesbianism, or oral sex. If questions arise on these issues, be discreet, keeping in mind that for the young women who are less exposed, too much information can be as dangerous as too little. Make time to counsel in private with those who ask for guidance in these areas.

Balance fun with purpose and enjoy coaching the young women in purity!

SUGGESTIVE SESSION FORMAT

- Opening Prayer
- Ice Breaker (For example: What does a young woman and a private garden have in common? *Private Gardens*, Chapter 5)
- Repeat Theme Text together.
- Assign each member one Bible verse to read when appropriate. (Do this again when each one has had a turn to read.)
- Lead out in the discussion encouraging participation. Steer the discussion toward the fulfillment of the lesson objective(s) stated at the beginning of the chapter.
- Stress *Points To Remember* or ask members to share the points they consider interesting.
- Announce next meeting or any activity you would like them to carry out.
- Closing Prayer. (Another opportunity for circle member participation.)

THE PURITY PLEDGE CEREMONY

Parents and supporters are encouraged to attend the short but meaningful ceremony. Make the service special by posting announcements or sending invitations. Add elegance to the presentation by having the young women wear a certain color or by providing them with corsages. Boost their self-esteem by allowing them to participate in the service.

Hand out commitment cards (See page 7) to the youth and adults at the beginning of the program. Have the pastor/speaker tell them when to sign after the purity message.

SUGGESTED SERVICE

- Musical Prelude/Congregational Songs/Selected Items by Pledgees
- Welcome and Occasion
- Scripture and Prayer
- Short Purity Message/Charge
- Presentation of the Purity Circle Members
- Individual Recital of Purity Verses
- The Youth Commitment in Unison
- The Adult Commitment in Unison
- Prayer of Dedication

Candles or any embellishments are at the discretion of the program planners. A fellowship reception afterwards, is appropriate.

COMMITMENT CARDS[1]

Purity Circle Pledge

Believing that God wants me to live a pure life,
I make a commitment to Him,
myself, my family, my friends, my future husband,
and my future children to a lifetime of purity.
I surrender my thoughts, my attitude, my conduct,
and my relationships to the purity of Christ.
I will encourage and support my Purity Circle friends
as we walk together in the purity lifestyle
from this day forward.

Signed:_____ Date:_____

Purity Circle Parent Pledge

Believing that God wants me to live pure,
I join _____,
in committing to a lifestyle of purity.
I make a commitment to God,
myself, my family, and my community of faith to abstain
from pornography, impure touching and conversations,
and sex outside a biblical marriage relationship
from this day forward.

Signed:_____ Date:_____

---

1   Adapted in part from *True Love Waits*® with permission from LifeWay Christian Resources.

FOLLOW-UP AND FEEDBACK

Purity Circle organizers would like to receive feedback concerning your group's response to the workbook material. We would also like to hear about activities in your group.

Communication with Purity Circle organizers can be assigned to an elected group leader who may also be responsible for scheduling regular follow-up meetings. Only members who have completed the workbook and taken the Purity Pledge can become group leaders.

Please send reports, questions, suggestions, or requests for follow-up materials to PurityCircle@usa.com.

We'd love to have you download our catalog of
titles we publish at:

www.TEACHServices.com

or write or email us your thoughts,
reactions, or criticism about this
or any other book we publish at:

TEACH Services, Inc.
254 Donovan Road
Brushton, NY 12916

info@TEACHServices.com

or you may call us at:

518/358-3494